SUSSEX ELECTORS

1832

Transcribed and Published by

PBN Publications

1992

Published by
PBN Publications
22 Abbey Road
Eastbourne
Sussex BN20 8TE

Introduction by Mr Brion Purdey
Principal Librarian, Hastings

INTRODUCTION

"I never saw such shocking bad hats in all my life" remarked the
disgusted Duke of Wellington as he surveyed the members of the
newly reformed House of Commons. By many of his less exalted
contemporaries, however, 1832 was regarded as the democratic
"annus mirabilis" of its age, a date to be ranked in importance
with 1265 and 1641. But just as De Montfort's "Parlement" and
the "Grand Remonstrance" might now be thought of as sounding but
a hollow clarion call for the advance of the common man or woman
so the Great (or First) Reform Act appears from this distance in
time to mark but a very small step forward along the road to
universal sufferage. One indeed might have cause to wonder at
the wild enthusiasm that swept the land at its passing onto the
Statute Book!

The number of actual voters had grown, it is true, but
insubstantially to our modern eyes. In ancient boroughs
enfranchised freemen numbered in tens had been replaced by
property qualified electorates counted still only in hundreds,
while in the counties the extension of the franchise to the £10
copyholders and longlease holders and the £50 shortlease holders
and tenants-at-will did not add so enormously to a voting
population which had been made up of 40/- freeholders (male and
over twenty one of course) since 1429. As example the parish of
Ashburnham had three electors in 1820 and twelve in 1822 while
Ditchling mustered seven and fifteen for the same years.

Yet for all that to those interested in the history and
development of any constituency, be it urban or rural, the names
of these newly enfranchised few, contained in published lists of
Registered Electors, possess considerable fascination. Such
lists, produced before the Ballot Act of 1872, including as they
do the details of votes cast, are calculated to delight the
hearts of students of political, local and family history alike
and here in the register published following the election of that
first ill-hatted Parliament, we have, not only details of
individuals, their parishes of residence and how they voted, but
also, since the original copy from which this book has been made
was an annotated "working" one, much additional information
relating to the political persuasion and influence then operating
in the County of Sussex.

/cont..

Observations on the loyalties, obligations and dependability of individual voters abound:-

> "Blacksmith employed and under the influence of Lord Ashburnham"; "Tory but promised at last election not to vote against Mr. Cavendish"; "Will go with the Majority"; "A man of no principle" and (referring to the Electorate of Hove) "the voters of this Parish are all independent".

More general comments, all apparently in the same hand and relating to the overall party affiliations of the various political agencies within the constituency, are to be found at the beginning of the register. "Brighton Agency - Mr. Cav's Principles are generally approved of by the Liberals. A Tory will never poll many votes at Brighton". "Hailsham Agency - the agricultural voters would with very few Exceptions be influenced by the Respective Landlords or others ...."

In this list of electors then, we have more than just the official record of a contest held at one of the most crucial times in the history of our Parliamentary system, we have a most revealing snapshot of the operation of influence at the hustings and, through it, we may note how even the most zealous adherents of reform themselves were quite easy in mind at the use of such pressure for what they, no doubt, regarded as the best of motives. As just one example take Sir Godfrey Webster, ardent advocate of change, who brought the news of the passing of the Great Reform Act from London to Battle and on to Hastings. The annotation of our register says of him - "Independent in principle - 27 in Pocket."!

Brion Purdey
Principal Librarian, Hastings

ii

ABBREVIATIONS

Chas........Charles
Col.........Colonel
Dan.........Daniel
Fredk.......Frederick
Gen.........General
Gent........Gentleman
Hon.........Honorable
Ind.........Independent
IOW.........Isle of Wight
Jas.........James
jun.........junior
Lieut.......Lieutenant
Matt........Matthew
Mr Cav......Mr Cavendish (this abbreviation is used in the
            original)
sen.........senior
Thos........Thomas
T. Wells....Tunbridge Wells(Kent)
Wm..........William

VOTES The votes cast have been entered after the elector's name
CAST: using the following numerical code:
       Number 1 = A vote for Cavendish.
       Number 2 = A vote for Curteis.
       Number 3 = A vote for Darby.

NOTES: Parish of Registration is entered in () brackets when it
       is different from that of the Parish in which the person
       resides
       *Entries in italic print did not vote either through death
       or loss of qualification*
       Words inserted by the transcriber are in {} brackets
       Entries in [] have been deleted in the original text

ACKNOWLEDGMENT
PBN Publications wish to acknowledge the help and advice given by
Mr Roger Davey - County Archivist - East Sussex Record Office, to
Mr Brion Purdey for the introduction, and Mr David Chant for the
front cover illustration.

SUSSEX ELECTORS - 1832

A list of the registered electors and votes polled at 1832 election in Sussex

---

NOTES The Names of the Electors are arranged alphabetically in the Places in which the Electors reside. The Parishes etc., in East Sussex are placed first, in Alphabetical Order, then follow West Sussex, Kent, Surrey, London and Distant Places.

Where any Elector is not registered in the Place in which he resides, the Parish in which he is registered is placed opposite to his name.

The voters marked thus * polled on the second Day.

The Names of such as did not poll are printed in Italics - Of these persons, several were dead, and many others had lost their Qualifications.

It is probable that several of the Names are mis-spelt, which arises from the Inaccuracies in the Lists delivered in by the Overseers.

There are hand written observations as follows:-

The following general Observations have been made by the Agents.

BRIGHTON AGENCY - Mr Cav's Principles are generally approved by the Liberals. A Tory will never poll many Votes at Brighton. Another Year the Number of Voters will be nearly doubled in Consequence of many Omissions in registering on the last Occasion which will not be the Case again.

EAST GRINSTEAD AGENCY - The prinicpal Part of the Voters in Maresfield would wish to follow Mr Shelley as far as they well can and who is (notwithstanding they do not altogether agree in Politicks extremely well disposed toward Mr Cavendish. With respect to Fletching the principal Part of the Tenantry hold under Lord Sheffield who likewise has the same Feelings towards Mr Cav. But in all the Parishes in this Agency there is a very large Number of independent Voters who will not allow themselves to be swayed by their Landlords.

HAILSHAM AGENCY - The agricultural Voters would with very few Exceptions be influenced by their Respective Landlords or others. With Respect to the others they would vote according to their respective Inclinations in fact that in Case of a future contested Election Mr Cav would be reelected altho' opposed by a much more influential Tory Candidate than Mr Darby.

HORSHAM AGENCY - The only Instance in this Agency in which the Tenants were required by their Landlords to vote as they pleased was in Slaugham Parish. The Tenants of Mr Sergison were desirous of voting for Mr Cav but were prevented by an Order from him to give single Votes to Mr Curteis. With this Exception the Voters throughout this Agency who supported Mr Cav were influenced by any other motive than an Approval of his political Principals and Mr Stedman feels confident the Rank and Wealth of Mr Cav coupled with the known Liberality of and Consistency of his Character will ensure him in future the universal Support he received at the recent Election.

LEWES AGENCIES - The Voters in these Agencies are generally liberal.

TUNBRIDGE WELLS AGENCY - Many of the Tenants at Will are quite Independent of their Landlords and many of them voted at the last Election so as to shew clearly that the Time is gone by when Tenants are to be influenced by their Landlords. In fact at the present Day there is such a Want of good and substantial Tenants that Landlords are very cautious how they act towards them. The Tenant knowing there are plenty of Farms in the Market. The Outvoter in Kent being all or the Greater Part of them Freeholders may be considered as likely hereafter to vote according to the Dictates of their own Consciences. It should be observed in Reference to the Tenants of Lord Abergavenny in and near this Place that had they not been requested by Mr Rowland to vote as they did they would most of them done so as the general Feeling is very strong in favour of Mr Cav as well as Mr Curteis.

The Nomination took place at Lewes, on Tuesday the 18th day of December, 1832, at which William Courthope MABBOTT, Esq presided, as Deputy for Alexander DONOVAN, Esq., Sheriff of the County

2

The Nominations at Lewes on Tuesday 18th December, 1832.

Herbert Barratt Curteis, Esq., of Peasmarsh.
The Hon Charles Compton Cavendish of Compton Place.
George Darby Esq., of Markly.

On Monday 24th on casting up the Poll, the numbers were declared to be, for

The Hon Charles Compton Cavendish	2,388
Herbert Barratt Curteis, Esq	1,941
Mr Darby	668

Whereupon the Sheriff declared that the two former were duly elected.

LIST OF SUSSEX ELECTORS - 1832
E.S.R.O. Ref: AMS 6216

NAME   NAME OF LANDLORD AND/OR OBSERVATIONS

ALCISTON - 3

FEARS Thomas/12
RIDGE Henry/12   General Trevor's & Lord Gage's Tenant
STEPHENS William/12

ALDRINGTON

None resident

ALFRISTON - 18

BODLE John/12   Tenant of Earl Ashburnham, removed to
                                Wartling
BROOKER Charles/12
BROOKER Charles Springate/12
COOLEY Joseph/12
HARYOTT Richard/12
HASTING Henry/12
HILTON Richard/12
JENNER Thomas/12
KIDD William/12
MARCHANT Thomas Relf/12
MARCHANT William/1
NEWMAN Richard/12
PAGDEN Henry/12   Tenant of Earl Burlington

NAME	NAME OF LANDLORD AND/OR OBSERVATIONS
REEDS William/12	
SMITH Jesse/12	
WINCH Ralph/12	
WOODHAMS John/12	
WOODHAMS William/12	Tenant of Col Goldfinch, will not be influenced by his Landlord

ARDINGLY - 7

BETCHLEY Richard/12
COMBER Richard/12
COMBER Thomas/12
CROUCHER Richard/12

These voters promised their votes to Mr Cavendish approving his principles and were I believe uninfluenced.

FIEST James	became disqualified by leaving his Farm
HAMILTON Rev James/13	a Tory
PICKE James/3	in the employment of Mr Peyton

ARLINGTON - 18

ADE Charles/13	
BARBER John/12	
BARBER William/12	
BODLE Charles/1	
BODY James/12	
CHILD Thomas/1	Earl Plymouth
CRUTTENDEN Leonard/13	
CRUTTENDEN William/13	
FEARS George/12	
FOX Arthur/12	
FOX Cornelius/12	
GOSDEN Thomas/13	Earl of Plymouth
GOWER William/12	
GUTSELL William/12	
HIDE William jun/12	
HIDE William sen/1	Colonel Goldfinch, will not be influenced
PAGDEN Thomas/12	
TUTT John/13	

ASHBURNHAM - 12

BEENEY Samuel/12	Miller. Independent
COOKE Edward/3	Tenant of Lord Ashburnham

NAME	NAME OF LANDLORD AND/OR OBSERVATIONS
GEERING George(Westham)	*Blacksmith. Employed by and under influence of Lord Ashburnham*
HILDER Benjamin	*Tenant of Lord Ashburnham's*
LEMMON William/23	Influenced by Lord Ashburnham but of liberal politics
MARTIN John/2	Tenant of Mr Gregory
NOAKES Thomas/3	Tenant of Lord Ashburnham
PENNINGTON William/13	Tenant of Lord Ashburnham
PINYON James/12	Tenant of Henry Dorset Esq, Freshwater IOW. Independent.(see"Distant Places")
SMITH Henry/12	Tenant of Lord Ashburnham
VENESS Isaac/23	Tenant of Lord Ashburnham
WARNEFORD Rev Edward/3	Under influence of Lord Ashburnham

BALCOMBE - 16

BONES William/12	Independent
BOOKER John	*Postmaster*
BROWN Joseph/12	Independent
COMBER John/12	Tenant of Mrs Chatfield
COMBER Thomas	*Tenant of Mrs Chatfield who requested him to vote for Mr Cav. & Mr Darby*
CROUCHER Thos/1(Cuckfield)	Bailiff to Mrs Chatfield
GIBB John/12	Independent
GIBB Thomas/12	Independent
HUMPHREY Michael/12	Independent
MARTIN Stephen(Keymer)	*Independent*
NEWNHAM William/1	Independent
SAREL Rev Henry Rule*/3	
STENNING Edward/12	Tenant of Mrs Chatfield
TESTER Charles/12	Tenant of Sir Timothy Shelley
TURNER William/12	Tenant of Mrs Chatfield
WEBBER John/12	Independent

BARCOMBE - 14

ALLEN Rev Robert/13	
AWCOCK George/12	Lost his qualification
BROOK James sen/12(Newick)	Sir Charles Goring, influenced by Mr Jenner
CONSTABLE John	*Captain Richardson*
COPPARD James*/13	Captain Richardson
COX Thomas/12	Lord Liverpool's Reeve, influenced by Mr Jenner
FULLER James/12	Sir G Shiffner
FUNNELL James/12	Mr Wood, Brewer, influenced by Mr Fuller

5

NAME	NAME OF LANDLORD AND/OR OBSERVATIONS
HOLROYD John Borrett	*Mr Jenner's Son in Law*
JENNER Richard sen/12	Independent
KNIGHT Richard jun*/12 (Hamsey)	T Partington Esq
SMYTH George/12	Independent
WESTGATE William/12	B Ridge
WIGNEY George/12	Influenced by Mr Jenner

BATTLE - 59

ALDERTON Henry	*Innkeeper. Independent*
BADCOCK Thomas sen/12	Independent
BARTON Thomas*/13	Clerk to the Battle Bench of Magistrates, influenced by their Tory Clients
BELLINGHAM Thos Charles/13	Clerk to the Battle Bench of Magistrates, influenced by their Tory Clients
BENEY George/13	Independent
BIRCH Rev Thomas D D/13	Dean of Battle, a Tory
BRISCOE Wastel/13	Independent but a Tory
BRYANT Richard/12	Independent
BURGESS James/12	Independent
BURGESS John/12	Independent
CHRISTMAS Robert/3	Independent. Tenant of Sir G Webster
COCKETT George/12	Independent
COCKETT Richard	*Independent*
COMFORT James	*Independent*
CHRISTFORD Robert/2	Independent
CUTHBERT John*/12	Independent
ELDRIDGE John/3	Independent
ELDRIDGE Robert/12	Independent Tenant of Sir G Webster
ELDRIDGE Thomas*/12	Independent
EMARY Charles*/12	George Inn. Tenant of T Breeds of Hastings
FRANKS John*/12	Independent. works under Mr Laurence
GARNER William/12	Independent. Dissenting Minister
GANSDEN Charles/1(All Saints Hastings)	Independent
GIBBS William/13	Independent
GOODWIN Charles*/12	Independent
GOWER James/12	Independent
HAMMOND Charles Sampson/12	Independent
HUNT Thomas/3	Tenant of Earl Ashburnham
KELL Nathaniel Polhill	*Mr Darby's Agent*
KENWARD John/12	Independent
LANDSDELL James/12	Independent

NAME	NAME OF LANDLORD AND/OR OBSERVATIONS
LAURENCE Charles*/12	Independent
LAURENCE Charles jun*/12	Independent
MANN Matthew/12	Independent. Publican
MARTIN Edwin(Hooe)	*Mr Curteis's Agent. Mr Cavendish's*
MARTIN James	*Mr Curteis's Agent 1820*
MATTHIS Thomas/1	Independent
METCALF George/12	Independent
METCALF William/12	Independent
NEVE William/12	Independent
NOAKES William/12	Independent
PATCHING James/12	Independent. Tenant of Sir G Webster's
PEARSON Richard/12	Independent
QUAIFE James/3	Goverment(sic) Pensioner late of Hackney Coach Office. Tenant of Sir G Webster
QUAIFE Thomas/3	Tenant with his father
SARGENT George*/12	Independent
SHAW John*/12	Independent
SLATTER George*/12	Independent
SPRAY James/3	Ind. Tenant of Sir G Webster and in partnership with William Ticehurst
TAYLOR Arthur/12	Independent
TAYLOR Stephen/12	Independent
THORPE George/12	Independent
TICEHURST William/3	Parish Clerk and under the influence of the Dean
WALKER Adam/13	Independent
WATTS James/13	Surgeon. Independent
WATTS Robert	*Surgeon. Ind. Brother in Law to Mr Barton*
WEBSTER Sir Godfrey, bart	*Independent in principle(27 in Pocket*
WELLER William*/12	Independent
WORGE John/1	Ind. Uncle of Mr Duke Mr Cavendish's Agent

BECKLEY - 28

BAKER William/12(Peasmarsh)
BAKER William sen/12
BOWLIN Thomas/12
COOPER Benjamin/12
COOPER Charles/12
COOPER Stephen/12
ELFICK Thomas/12
FAIRHALL John/12

NAME	NAME OF LANDLORD AND/OR OBSERVATIONS
FAIRHALL William/12	
GILBERT James/12	
GILBERT John/12	
GILBERT Thomas/12	
HOLLANDS William/12	
KING Richard/12	
NORRIS John/12	
PARSONS Humphrey/12	
PARSONS James/12	

Nearly all the {above} Voters are Tenants to, or in Mr
Curteis's Interest, and all are Whigs.

POILE Henry/12	Disqualified
REEVES Thomas Walter	*Tory*
RUGG George	*Tory*
RUSSELL John/12	Whig
SELMES Samuel*/12	Whig
STONHAM James/12	Tenant to Edward Pennyfather Esq
STONHAM Thomas/23	Tenant to Edward Pennyfather Esq
STONHAM Thomas/23	Tenant to Edward Pennyfather Esq
THAMSETT John/12	Whig in Mr Curteis's Interest
VINSETT James/12	Whig in Mr Curteis's Interest
WYBOURNE Stephen/12	Whig in Mr Curteis's Interest

BEDDINGHAM - 2

HART Richard sen/12 (Uckfield)	Lord Gage
JENNER John/12	General Trevor

BERWICK - 5

DULY Henry/12	Mr Stace
SAXBY Richard Scrace/12	Lord Gage
STACE William/12	John Fuller Esq
WESTGATE William/12	Mr Stace
WHITE Henry/12	Mr Stace

BEXHILL - 48

The chief Landowners in this Parish are the Lords
Plymouth, Chichester, and Messrs Fuller, Rose, Hill,
Gordon/Broomwick, Stafford, Moorman/Bexhill/Camac/
Hastings/Cranstone/E. Grinstead/Pelham, Crowhurst
Park/the majority of the Voters are under no direct
influence and certainly at present opposed to Toryism.

Several of them are small owners - There is no one
Landlord who possesses great power and generally speaking
they are not likely to interfere. Had the contest at the
last Election been between Mr Cavendish and Mr Curteis the
Parish was rather more favourable to the latter Gent than
the former as being more known to them, this objection
will however be removed at the next Election.

NAME	NAME OF LANDLORD AND/OR OBSERVATIONS
BAKER Rev Thomas/13	
BARTON John/1	
BEECHING Samuel/12	
BEECHING Thomas/12	
BEECHING William/12	
BREETON Thomas/12	
BROOK Arthur	
BROOK John Charles(Burwash)	
BROOKS Stephen/12	
CRISMAS Stephen/12	
CRISMAS Thomas/12	
COALMAN Samuel/12	
CROWHURST John/12	
CRUTTENDEN John/12	
CURTISS William/12	
DALLAWAY Thomas/12	
DAWES Edward/12	
DAY Richard/2	
DEUDNEY James/12	
DEVALL Thomas/12	
DUKE Thomas/12(Wartling)	
DUKE Walter	
HAMMOND Thomas/12	
HOLLAND Samuel/12	
LANSDELL Edward/12	
LARKIN Thomas/12	
MATHIS Richard/12	
MILLER Thomas/12	
OLIVER James/12	
OSBORN Lavett/12	
PARKER John/12	
PELLING Dearing/12	
PRIOR Edward/12	
RANSOM Stephen/12	
REEVES Henry/12	
RICH Henry/12	
RUSSELL James/12	

NAME	NAME OF LANDLORD AND/OR OBSERVATIONS
RUSSELL William/12	
SINDEN John/12	
SINDEN Samuel	
SINDEN Thomas/12	
SMITH Peter	
STRIDE Robert/12	
THOMAS George/12	
THOMAS James/12	
THOMAS Stephen/12	
THOMAS William/12	
YOUNG Isaac/12	

BISHOPSTONE - 3

CATT William/12	uninfluenced
COOPER Thomas/12	uninfluenced
FARNCOMBE George/13	uninfluenced

BLATCHINGTON(EAST) - 3

KING John/13	uninfluenced
LEWIS Rev John/3	uninfluenced
SAMPSON William King/13	uninfluenced

BLATCHINGTON(WEST) - 1

HODSON William/12

BODIAM - 5

BISHOP John/3	Farmer. Mr Davis. Independent
BODY John/12	Farmer & Miller. Independent
BUCKLAND James/12	Farmer. Independent
SHOOSMITH John/12	Blacksmith. Himself. wishes to please his Customers
THOMAS Rev Sir John Godfrey, bart*/12	Rector. Independent

No particular Individual has influence in this Parish.

BOLNEY - 6

AGATE Thomas
ANSCOMBE Mark
CRAGG Richard
JEFFERY Richard/12
PIERCE Stephen
WINTER William/12

NAME	NAME OF LANDLORD AND/OR OBSERVATIONS
	BREDE - 21
ADES John	*Tenant of F Furner Esq*
APPS William/12	Whig
AUSTIN Thomas	*Tenant F Furner Esq*
BAKER James/12	Whig
BLAKE Stephen/12	Whig
BOURNE Francis	*Tenant of F Furner Esq*
BOURNE John/12	Tenant of Tory Landlord
CAMPBELL Harry/1	Whig
COLEMAN William jun/12	Whig
DITCH John*/1	Whig
HELE Rev Robert Selby/13	Tory
MERCER Robert*/12	Whig
PAIN Thomas*/12	Whig
RICHARDSON James/12	Whig
RICHARDSON Wakeham Thos/12	Whig
SKINNER James/12	Tenant of E Milward Esq
SMITH David/12	Whig
SMITH David jun/12	Tenant of E Milward Esq
SMITH Henry/12	Whig
TUCKER Thomas/12	Whig
YOUNG Richard/12	Whig

BRIGHTON - 299

In this Town there are very few Voters under any direct
Influence, The very great majority are of liberal
principles, many radically so.

ACKERSON Robert/1
ADE John(All Saints, Lewes)
AKEHURST Samuel/12
ALLEN Joseph/13
ALFREE James/12
ANDERSON Rev James Stuart Murray/13
ANDERSON Rev Robert/13
ATTREE George Thomas/12
ATTREE Thomas/12
ATTREE William*/12(Keymer)
ATTREE William Wakeford
BARNARD Nathaniel/13
BARNETT William/12
BASS Isaac*/12
BATES Henry William/13(Denton)
BATHO Matthew Robert/13

11

NAME	NAME OF LANDLORD AND/OR OBSERVATIONS

BEDFORD George*/12
BEEDHAM William
BELLINGHAM Charles/12
BENSON Thomas/13
BEST Thomas*/13(Ditcheling)
BEVES Edward/12
BEVES Samuel/12
BIGGS William/12
BILLINGSHURST Edward/12
BLABER Henry/12
BLABER William
BLACKLOCK William/13
BLAKER Harry/13(Portslade)
BLAKER John/12
BLUNT Sir Charles Richard, Bart*/1(Brighton,Ringmer & Heathfield)
BODLE Richard/12
BORRER John Hamlin(Bolney)
BOXALL William/13
BOYS Jacob/12(Hove)
BRADFORD Nenyon Masters/12
BRADSHAW John/13
BRINTON Robert Nineham/12
BROOKER Henry/12
BROWN Joseph/1
BUCKOLL Stephen/12
BUDD Henry
CAMP William Samuel
CARTER James*/12
CARTER Thomas*/12
CATT William jun/12
CHAFFEY Thomas*/12
CHALK John/12(Hove)
CHANDLER John/12
CHAPLIN William/1
CHAPMAN Henry/12
CHAPMAN Richard/12
CHASSEREAU George/12
CHATFIELD Charles/12
CHEESMAN George/12
CHEESMAN Harry/13
CHEESMAN James/12
CHEESMAN William/12
CHILDRENS John Cheesman/12
CHITTENDEN George/12
CHOYCE James/12

NAME	NAME OF LANDLORD AND/OR OBSERVATIONS

CLARK Samuel*/12

COBBY Charles

COLBATCH John/12

COLBRAN Harry Stiles/12

COLWILL Charles

COOPER Frederick*/1

COOPER Isaac/12

COOPER Robert Chester(All Saints, St John, St Michael, Cliffe, Southmalling & Southover)

COPPARD George(Westhoathly)

COPPARD James/12

CORDER Charles/12

CORDY James/13

CRIPPS Robert/12

CROSSWELLER Thomas/13

CROW Nathan

CULLEN James/12

DADLEY William Pearce/12

DALRYMPLE John Apsley(Mayfield)

DANCASTER George/12

DAVIS Benjamin*/13

DAVIS Richard/12

DIPLOCK John/12

DONNE Joseph/12

DOUBLEDAY William/12

DUMBRELL Charles/12

DUMBRELL James*/12

DURRANT William Mercer(Ticehurst)   *Had promised Mr Cav but was prevented going to Mayfield to poll on Account of ill Health*

EDWARDS Henry/12

EDWARDS Richard/12

ELLIS Frederick

ELLIS William/1

FAITHFULL George

FAITHFULL Henry

FIELD Joseph/12

FOSTER Edward

FRANCIS Samuel/12

FRANCIS Thomas/12

FREEMAN Thomas/13

FURNER William/13

GALLARD John/12

GARRATT John/12(Waldron)

GLAISYER John*/12

NAME	NAME OF LANDLORD AND/OR OBSERVATIONS

GOFFE John/12
GOOD John/12
GOODALL Thomas*/12
GORRINGE James/1(Patcham)
GOULTY John Nelson/12
GRANT Peter/2
GREEN Henry/12
GREEN Richard*/12
GREEN William*/12
GREENE Anthony Sheppey
GREGORY Richard Lemmon/12
GROVER John(Cliffe,Lewes)
GWYNNE George(All Saints,Lewes & Chiddingly)
HACK Daniel Prior*/12
HADDON Richard/12
HAINES Samuel/12
HALLETT William/12
HAMILTON Thomas/12
HAMLIN Thomas*/12
HANSON William
HARRINGTON George/13
HARRINGTON Thomas
HILL Edward/12
HOAD Richard/1
HOBBS Edward/12(Battle)
HODD Stephen Tutt
HODSON Thomas/13
HOLDEN Joseph Douglas/12
HOLFORD John/12
HOPE William/12
HOPPS John/12
HUGHES David/13
HUMPHREY Richard/12
HUMPHREY William/12
INMAN Richard/12
INMAN Thomas Atkins/12
IZARD John /13
JUDSON Henry/1
KEMP Grover*/12
KEMP Thomas Read/12
KENT Edward*/12
KING George/12
KIPPING William/13
KIRCHNER John/13
KNAPP John/12

NAME	NAME OF LANDLORD AND/OR OBSERVATIONS
LAMBERT William/12	
LAMPRELL Abraham Johnson/12	
LASHMAR John*/12	
LASHMAR Richard/12	
LEE Henry/12	
LEGG James/12	
LEMPRIERE Clement/12	
LOWDELL George/13(East Grinstead)	
MANSER Francis*/12(Brighton & Ditcheling(sic))	
MARSHALL Edmund/12(Brighton)	
MARSHALL John/12	
MARSHALL Richard/12	
MARTIN Henry/12	
MASQUERIER John James/12	
MAY Charles Coleman/13	
MICHELL James Charles*/13	
MILLER William Oliver	
MILLS James Henry/12	
MILLS John/12	
MILLS Thomas/12	
MOORE John	
MORLING John/1	
MORRIS Sergeant Witton/12	
MOTT Robert/12	
MUNN Thomas/12	
NEALL William/12	
NEWNHAM Richard/1	
OLIVE John/12	
OVER Thomas/12	
PACKHAM Thomas	
PALMER Edmund/12	
PALMER Thomas/12	
PANNETT Stephen/12	
PARSONS Henry/12	
PARSONS George/12	
PARSONS Joseph*/12	
PATCHING Richard jun*/12	
PAYNE Richard Kent/3	
PEDDAR Robert*/13	
PENFOLD William/12	
PENTICOST Thomas	
PHILLIPS John Francis/12	
PHILLIPSON John Bradshaw*/1	
PHILPOT Richard Price	
PICKFORD James	

NAME	NAME OF LANDLORD AND/OR OBSERVATIONS
PIKE James/12	
PINK Thomas/12	
POCOCK John*/1	
POCOCK John/13	
POCOCK John	
POCOCK John B/13	
POCOCK Thomas*/12	
POLLARD Francis/12	
POLLARD John/12	
POLLARD Philip/12	
POLLARD Thomas	
POUNE John/12	
PRICE Charles/13	
PROCTOR Rev G D D/13	Under Duke of Devonshire's influence
(St Michaels,Lewes)	through John Payne Collier Esq
PROSSER William	
RANGER Richard/1	
RANGER William/13	
REASON William/2	
REYNOLDS Charles/12	
REYNOLDS John/12	
RIDLEY Samuel/12	
ROBERTS Fleming Thomas/12	
ROBERTSON Archibald/12	
ROBISON James/1	
ROGERS Edward/12	
ROWLAND Joshua/12	
RUSBRIDGE Henry/12(Rottingdean)	
SANDERS Samuel Farncombe*/12	
SAUNDERS John	
SAUNDERS William	
SAVAGE Edmund/12	
SAWYER George/12	
SAWYER G William/12(Brighton & Hove)	
SAWYER John/12	
SCOTT Sir David, Bart/13	
SCUTT Thomas	
SEYMOUR William/12(Portslade)	
SHARP William/3	
SHIFFNER Thomas(Hamsey)	
SHRIVELL Cornelius/12	
SHUGGARS James/12	
SIVEWRIGHT James/13	
SMITH Horatio/12	
SMITH John/12	

NAME	NAME OF LANDLORD AND/OR OBSERVATIONS

SMITH John/12
SMITH Samuel/12
SMITH Stephen James/12
SMITH William/12
SMITH William/1
SMITHERS Henry/13
SPYRING John Samuel Shepheard/12
STEVENS William/12
STEWART Charles
STOCKS Matthew/12
STONE B J*/12(Brighton & Hove)
STONE James/12
STONE John/13
STONE Richard/13
STORROR Thomas/12
STUCKEY Richard/1
SUGGERS George/12
TAYLER Robert*/13
TAYLOR John/12
TESTER Richard/12
THOMPSON Richard/3
THORBY Thomas/1
THORNCROFT Samuel/12
THUNDER Carter/13
THUNDER Edward/12
TICEHURST Joseph/12
TILBRY Edward/2
TOWNER William/12
TRANGMAR John Tanner
TRANGMAR William/12
TUPPEN Harry/12
UPTON John/12
VALLANCE Edmund*/12
VALLANCE George/1
VALLANCE John jun
VENNER Ambrose/12
VERRALL Henry/12
VICK Christopher Wren/13
VIRGOE Samuel/12
WAGNER Rev Henry Michell/3(Brighton & West Blatchington)
WAITE Thomas/12
WALLS Joseph/12
WALLS William/12
WALTON William/12
WEAVER Joseph/12

NAME	NAME OF LANDLORD AND/OR OBSERVATIONS
WELLER Samuel/12	
WELSFORD Roger/12	
WEST Thomas/13	
WHICHELO Richard Lemon/12	
WIGNEY Isaac Newton/12	
WIGNEY Robert/12	
WIGNEY William jun/12	
WILDS Amon/13	
WILLARD Leonard Kilham/3(Arlington)	
WILLIAMS William/1	
WINGHAM Thomas	
WISDEN Thomas/12	
WOOD Benjamin/12	
WOOD George Edward	
WOODHAMS William/12	
WRIGHT Thomas Henry/13	
YEATES John/12	

BRIGHTLING - 7

Mr Fuller has the greatest Influence in this Parish but he is not disposed to exert himself about Elections.

FULLER John Esq	*Himself. Independent*
GOLDSMITH Benjamin/12	Farmer. J Fuller Esq. Independent
HAYLEY Rev John Burrel/13	Rector. Ind. Tory
HOLLAWAY John/12	Farmer. Independent
HOLLAWAY Thomas/12	Farmer's son. Independent
REYNOLDS Joseph/12	Farmer. J Fuller Esq. Independent
WESTOVER John/12(Burwash)	Farmer. Independent

BROOMHILL - NONE RESIDENT

BURWASH - 54

BAKER Anthony/12	Shoemaker. Himself. Independent
BAKER Edward/12	Shoemaker. Himself. Independent
BALDOCK John	*Solicitor. Himself. Mr Cavendish's Agent*
BLUNDEN John/12	Farmer. J Ellis Esq of Barning. Influenced by Landlord
BOURNER Charles	*Farmer. J Worge of Battle. Ind*
BROWN Stephen/12	Collarmaker. Himself. Independent
CANE James/12	Farmer. Mr Bishop. Independent
CHEESMAN Thomas*/12	Farmer. Himself. Independent
CROWHURST Robert/3	Shopkeeper. Himself. Ind. A Dissenter

18

NAME	NAME OF LANDLORD AND/OR OBSERVATIONS
CRUTTENDEN John/12	Farmer. Himself. Independent
CRUTTENDEN Samuel/12	Farmer. Rev W Curteis. Independent
DANN Jesse/1	Farmer. Himself. Independent
FLEMING John/12	Hairdresser. Himself. Independent
GILBERT George Fagg/12	Farmer. Himself. Independent
GOULD Rev Joseph	Curate. Rev Dr McKenzie. Independent
HAVILAND Henry Hone Esq/12	Ind. Himself. Deputy Chairman at Mayfield
HENTY John/12	Farmer. R S Appleyard Esq. Ind
HOOKER Richard/13	Shoemaker. Independent
HONEYSETT John/12	Miller. Himself. Independent
HOWE Matthew/12	Innkeeper. Mr Wood, Lewes. Ind
HYLAND David/3	Farmer. Rev J Constable. Influenced by his Landlord to vote for Mr Darby and by mistake ommitted to vote for Mr Cav
HYLAND Joseph*/12	Farmer. Mr Chelow. Independent
LADE James/12	Farmer. E J Curteis Esq. Ind
LANGRIDGE Stephen/12	Farmer. Himself. Independent
LEANEY James/1	Innkeeper. Himself. Independent
MANKTELOW Richard/12	Cabinetmaker. Himself. Independent
MANWARING William/12	Common Carrier. Himself. Independent
NEWINGTON John/12	Farmer. J Newington & H Playsted. Ind
NEWINGTON Samuel/12	Shoemaker. Himself. Independent
NOAKES James/12	Farmer. Edward Hussey Esq. Independent
NOAKES James/12	Farmer. Himself. Independent
NOAKES John/12	Clockmaker. Himself. Independent
OLIVER William/13	Farmer. Philcox & Baldock would not like to vote against the wishes of his Landlords
PARK John/12	Butcher. Himself. Independent
PARSONS William/12	Farmer. Himself. Independent
PHILCOX James	Solicitor. Himself. Mr Cavendish's Agent
PILBEAM Edmund/12	Glazier. Himself. Independent
PILBEAM James/3	Blacksmith. Himself. Independent
REEVES Richard/12	Bricklayer. Himself. Independent
RUSSELL Francis	Farmer, Independent. Rejected
RUSSELL Francis jun/12	Miller. Independent
RUSSELL Thomas/12	Farmer. Independent would not vote as Mr Hyland wish'd
SAWYER Joseph/12	Shopkeeper. Himself. Independent
SIMES Edward*/13	Farmer. Lord Ashburnham. wish'd to oblige his Landlord
SONE George/12	Shopkeeper. Himself. Independent

NAME	NAME OF LANDLORD AND/OR OBSERVATIONS
SUTTON John/12	Huxter. Himself. Independent
THOMPSON William/12	Bricklayer. Himself. Independent
VIGOR James	*Butcher. Ind. Intended to have voted for Cav & Cur*
VIGOR John/12	Butcher. His father J Vigor. Ind
WESTON Philip/13	Blacksmith. Himself. Independent
WINCHESTER William/13	Innkeeper. P Pope. Independent
WOOD Benjamin	*Himself. Carpenter a radical intended to have voted Cav & Cur*
WOOD John/12(Etchingham)	Shopkeeper. Richard Reeves. Lost his qualification
WOOD Richard/12	Himself. Shoemaker an Independent radical

BUXTED - 29

ALCHORN Thomas/3
BALDOCK William/12
BATCHELOR Henry/1
BENHAM George Spencer/12
BEST James/13
COE James/12
EWEN William/12
GILBERT Isaac/12   W F Hick Esq
GORRINGE William/12
HALL Benjamin/3
HEMSLEY John/3
HODSON Rev John/3
HOLMAN John/12
JARRATT John/1
NASH William/12
OLIVE John/12   an old fool
PAGE Edward/3
PIERCE George*/12
PIPER Robert/1
STANFORD William/13
STARR Thomas/1
SUSSANS Thomas/12
TAYLOR Richard
TULLY William/12
WATSON Edmund/12
WICKENS Samuel/3
WINTER James/3
WORDSWORTH Rev Christopher
WREN Thomas/12

NAME	NAME OF LANDLORD AND/OR OBSERVATIONS

CATSFIELD - 15

NAME	NAME OF LANDLORD AND/OR OBSERVATIONS
ADAMS James/12	Ind. Tenant to Col Pilkington(see below)
BEDINGFIELD Francis P/2	Independent
BONTOR Robert jun/12	Independent
CHRISMAS James/2	Tenant of J Fuller Esq
DAVIS Thomas	*Innkeeper. Independent*
FARMER James/12	Independent
FOARD John	*Under influence of Overseers*
HILDER Thomas/3(Northiam)	
LADE John Trill/3	Tenant of Col Pilkington but influenced by Mr Darby
PILKINGTON Andrew/12	Independent
PLUMBLEY Uriah/12	Independent
WATERS Benjamin/12	Independent
WATERS Richard	*Tenant of his father B Waters & J C Pelham Esq*
WRENN Benjamin*/12	Independent
WRENN Frederick/12	His son. Independent

CHAILEY - 23

NAME	NAME OF LANDLORD AND/OR OBSERVATIONS
ALCORN John/12	Independent
ANSCOMBE Allen/12	Independent
BEARD George/12	Independent. Tenant of Genl. St.John
BEARD John/12	Tenant of Genl. St.John
BEARD Thomas Rootes/12	Tenant of Mr Trebeck
BEST Gabriel/12	Tenant of Gen St.John
BRIERLY Frederick	*Tenant of Sir James Scarlett*
BROOK Henry/12	Independent
DUDENEY Edward/13	Tenant of Sir G Shiffer(sic)
HAMSHAR Harry/12	Independent
HEPBURN Maj Gen Francis/3	Independent
HOBDEN William/13	Tenant of Lord Sheffield
JONES David/12	Independent
KNIGHT Edward/12	Gen Hepburn & Sir James Scarlett
MORLEY James*/13	Tenant of Lord Sheffield
NORMAN Richard/12	
PANNETT Thomas/12	Tenant of Sir C Goring
ST.JOHN The Hon Frederick*/12	
TREBECK Rev Thomas*/1	Duke of Devonshire
URIDGE William/13	James Ingram
WALLS Joseph/12	Independent
WATERMAN Edward/12	Independent
WESTON Henry/12	Sir James Scarlett. Influenced by Mr Jenner

CHALVINGTON - 8

CARPENTER James/1
CARPENTER Thomas/12
FRENCH William/12
GUY Thomas/12
MARTEN Michael/12
MEDHURST Michael/12
PICKNELL Robert/12
VINE John/12

CHIDDINGLY - 26

BAXHILL John/12
COLLINS James/12(Southover)
DAY Thomas/3
DRAY Edward/3   Mr Day
DUNK James/12
FUNNELL Samuel
GOLDSMITH John/12
GUY David/12   Earl of Chichester
GUY George/12
GUY Thomas/12   Earl of Chichester
GUY William/12
HIDE Richard/12   Son of Mr Hide, Arlington
HOLMAN John/12   Will vote as Mr Lower thinks proper
HOLMAN Samuel/12   Will vote as Mr Lower thinks proper
HOLMAN William/12   Will vote as Mr Lower thinks proper
KNIGHT John/12   J Woodward
LOWER Richard/12
MORRIS Joseph/3(Laughton)
NOAKES George/12
PELLING Richard/12
REEVES Robert/3   Is connected with Mr Darby's Family
RUSSELL John Clifford/12   Votes with Mr Lower
SMITH Stephen/12
SOPER Richard/23
WESTON John/12
WHITE James/23   Employed by Mr Day

CHILTINGTON - 7

CRIPPS John Martin*/1   Independent
         Westmeston)
EGLES Edward/12   Independent
ELPHICK Samuel   *Sir G Shiffner*
FAULCONER Stephen Sawyer   *Sir James Scarlett*
MARTIN John/13   J M Cripps

NAME	NAME OF LANDLORD AND/OR OBSERVATIONS
URIDGE Henry/12	Sir James Scarlett
WOOD Richard/12	Independent

CLAYTON - 11

AVERY Thomas/12
BROOKER William/12
BURTON John/12(Clayton & Brighton)
EDE John
FOARD Thomas sen/12
GAINSFORD John/12
HALLIWELL Rev Henry/3
JEFFERY James/12
OCKENDEN William/13
STUBBS Hasted
WHITEMAN Thomas Dominick/12

CRAWLEY - 8

BISSHOPP Robert/12	Independent
BROADWOOD Thomas	*If at home would have voted for Mr Cavendish*
MIDDLETON Charles/12	Independent
MITCHEL John/12	Independent
NEWMAN James/12	Independent
ROBISON John/12	Independent
SNELLING James/12	Independent
TUSLER James/13	Independent

CROWHURST - 3

REEVE Thomas/23	Tenant of Richard King Sampson Esq of Hailsham
RUSH Rev Henry John/13	A Tory. Curate of the Rev Sir Charles Hardinge of Tunbridge Wells
WOOD William/13	Tenant of George Hooper Esq of Lewes

CUCKFIELD - 49

AGATE Thomas/13
BANNISTER John*/2
BANNISTER William*/2
BARBER Philip/12
BEST Faulkner/12
BRAY Henry/12
BRAY Henry*/2
BRIGDEN Thomas*/2
BROOMFIELD Thomas
CAFFYN Jacob

CHERRY John Peter*/12
COOK John English
DURRANT William/12
ELLIOTT William/12
FIELD James/12
FIELDWICK William*/2
FORD William/12
GREENFIELD Edmund
HALL William/12
HALL William/12
HOBDEN James/12
JEFFERY Joseph*/2
JEFFERY Joseph jun*/2
JENNER Charles/12
JUNIPER Charles/12
KENNARD Richard/12
KNIGHT Stephen/12
LENEY Isaac/12
MARCHANT William/13
MITCHELL John/12
NORMAN James Ormond/1
PACKHAM John*/2
PACKHAM Richard*/2
PACKHAM William*/2
PAGET Henry
PENFOLD Philip*/2
PENNIFOLD Michael*/2
POTTER Peter/12
SERGISON Warden
SMITH William/12(St. John, Lewes)
TAYLOR George*/2
TAYLOR William*/2
UPTON Stephen*/2
UPTON William/12
WALLER Samuel
WELLS Sir John K.C.B.
WILEMAN John/12
WOOD Stephen/12
WOOLVEN Richard/12

DALLINGTON - 11

BLUNDEN Andrew/12   Farmer. Independent/since removed
BOURNER Peter/3   Farmer. Himself. Independent
HONEYSETT John/12   Shopkeeper. Independent
MARCHANT Thomas/23   Farmer. Lord Ashburnham. Ind

NAME	NAME OF LANDLORD AND/OR OBSERVATIONS
PETERS John/12	Shopkeeper. Independent
RANDOLL John/3	Gentleman. Himself. Ind. a Tory
SANDS George/12	Farmer. Independent
SAWYER John/12	Yeoman. Independent
TAYLOR Samuel	*Farmer. Lord Ashburnham, would not like to go against Landlord's wishes*
TRILL John	*Parish Clerk. Independent*
VENESS John/23	Farmer. Lord Ashburnham, would not like to go against Landlord's wishes

DENTON - 1

PUTLAND William/12	Uninfluenced

DITCHELING - 15

BODDINGTON Robert/3	A Tory
BROWN James/12	Mr Cavendish's Canvasser
COMBER Thomas/12	Under influence of Mr Brown
DEAN John/12	Independent a liberal
ELLIOTT William/12	Independent
GRINYER Thomas/12	Independent
ILLMAN Thomas/12	Independent
KENSETT Jesse/12	Independent
MERCER Richard/12	Independent
MICHELL John/12	Independent
MUDDLE Thomas	*Came to Lewes to vote for Mr Cavendish but omitted to Poll*
ROWLAND Peter jun/12	Independent a liberal
TESTER Thomas/12	Independent
TURNER James/12	Independent
WOOD John/12	Independent

EASTBOURNE - 74

ALLCHORNE Richard/12 (Rotherfield)	Uninfluenced
BAKER Thomas/1	Tenant of the Earl of Burlington
BAKER William/1	Tenant of the Earl of Burlington
BOYS William/12(All Saints, Hastings)	Leasehold Tenant of the Earl of Burlington & D Gilbert Esq
BRIDGER John/1	Influenced by D Gilbert Esq
BOOTH Robert*/3	A Strong Tory
BROWN Joseph/12	Influenced by Lord Burlington & D Gilbert Esq, Lords of Eastbourne
BUTCHER John/12	Tenant of D Gilbert Esq
CALDECOTT Richard Matthias /12	Uninfluenced
CAPLIN Henry/1	Uninfluenced

NAME	NAME OF LANDLORD AND/OR OBSERVATIONS
COLMAN John/12	Tenant of the Earl of Burlington
COOPER Rev George Miles/1 (Eastbourne & St. Leonards, Hastings)	Chaplin to the Earl of Burlington
COPPARD Dennis/1	Uninfluenced
COPPARD Richard/1	Uninfluenced
COPPARD Richard jun/1	Uninfluenced
DOBREE Samuel*/12	Uninfluenced
DUMBRILL Edward/12	Tenant of the Lords of Eastbourne
DUMBRILL John Neville/12	Tradesman to the Earl of Burlington
DUMBRILL William/12	Tenant of the Lords of Eastbourne
FILDER James/1(Westham)	Tenant of the Earl of Burlington
FILDER Joseph/12(Wartling)	Tenant of the Earl of Burlington
FORD Henry/12	Tenant of the Lords
FILDER Moses/1(Pevensey)	Tenant of the Earl of Burlington
FREDERICK Thomas/3	Influenced by Major Willard
FRENCH William/1	Uninfluenced
GILBERT Davies/12	Uninfluenced
GORRINGE John/12	Tenant of the Earl of Burlington
GORRINGE John Pennington/12 (Pevensey)	Tenant of W Gilbert Esq
GRAYHAM John/2	Brother in Law to Mr Curteis
HART George/1	Tradesman to the Earl of Burlington
HART Richard/13	Influenced by Major Willard
HEATHFIELD William/12	Tradesman to the Earl of Burlington
HEATHURLY John*/12	Tenant of the Lords
HURST George/12	Tradesman of the Earl of Burlington
HURST Harry/12	Uninfluenced
HURST Robert/1	Uninfluenced
HURST Thomas/1	Tenant of the Earl of Burlington
HUSSELL John/1	Tenant of the Lords
HYLAND William/12	Influenced by D Gilbert Esq
JONES William/1	Tradesman of the Earl of Burlington
LANYON John Jenkinson*/1	Uninfluenced
LINDFIELD Peter/12(Ninfield)	Assistant Overseer of Eastbourne
MANDY James Caldicott/1	Tradesman of the Earl of Burlington
MANN John/12	Uninfluenced
MAYNARD George/1	Tradesman of the Earl of Burlington
MOCKETT Richard/1(Jevington)	Uninfluenced
MORRIS William/12	Tradesman of the Earl of Burlington
NEWMAN James/1	Tenant of the Earl of Burlington
NEWMAN John/1	Uninfluenced
NEWMAN William/12	Uninfluenced
NOAKES John/1	Tenant of the Lords
PAGDEN James/1	Tenant of the Earl of Burlington

NAME	NAME OF LANDLORD AND/OR OBSERVATIONS
PITMAN Rev Thomas/1	Uninfluenced
PRODGER William jun/12	Tradesman of the Earl of Burlington
PRODGER William sen/1	Tradesman of the Earl of Burlington
RAWDEN Charles Wyndham/12	Uninfluenced
REED John/1	Influenced by the Tenants of the Earl of Burlington
REED Richard	*Tenant of the Earl of Burlington*
RICHARDSON John/12	Uninfluenced
ROW John/12	Uninfluenced
STARR John/12(Waldron)	In service of D Gilbert Esq
STONE Richard Buckley/1	Tradesman of the Earl of Burlington
STRETTON John/13	Influenced by Major Willard
SUTTON William/1	Tradesman of the Earl of Burlington
THORNCROFT James/12	Influenced by D Gilbert Esq
TOWNER James/12	Influenced by D Gilbert Esq
TURNER Joseph*/12	Uninfluenced
TURNER William/12(Brighton)	Uninfluenced
VINE Thomas/12	Uninfluenced
WAYMARK John/1	Tradesman of the Earl of Burlington
WATERS Benjamin/12	Tenant of D Gilbert Esq
WEBSTER John Charles/1	Steward of Compton Place
WILLARD John Harry	*Tory but promised at last Election not to vote against Mr Cavendish*
WILLARD Nicholas*/13	Tory

EAST DEAN - 6

ASHBY George/13(Friston)	Tenant of the Earl of Liverpool
GARDENER Rev Christopher/13	Uninfluenced
HILLS John William/12	Influenced by Lord Liverpool's Tenants
HODSON James/12	Tenant of D Gilbert Esq
SCRASE Richard/12	Tenant of Lord Liverpool
WILLARD Charles/12	Uninfluenced

EAST GRINSTEAD - 102

AGATE William/2	Tenant of Robert Crawford Esq, a Conservative
ALDRIDGE Rev William/12	
BAILEY William/13	
BANKIN George	
BARBER Henry*/12	
BETCHLEY Richard/13	Mr Peerless. a Liberal
BETCHLEY Thomas*/12	
BLACKSTONE Henry/13	
BLACKSTONE John/3	
BLUNT Joseph/13	

NAME	NAME OF LANDLORD AND/OR OBSERVATIONS
BOND Thomas/12	
BOWRAH John/1	John Biddulph Esq. Liberal
BROOKER Benjamin/3	
BUDGEN Thomas/13	
BURT Thomas Robert	
CADDELL Philip/12	
CHAPMAN Benjamin/12	
CHAPMAN William/12	
CHARLWOOD Thomas/12	
CLARK John Calvert*/13	
COLLINS John/12	
COLLINS Miles Bailey/1	
COMBER William jun/1	
COTTON Abraham*/1	Mr Wood. Liberal
CRANSTON Edward/12	Edward Cranston Esq. Friend of Mr Cavendish's
CRAWFORD Robert/3	Robert Crawford Esq. Conservative
CUTLER John/12	Mr Kelsey. Liberal
EDGAR John	*Mr Edgar. Liberal*
ELLIS George/12	
ELPHICK Edward/12	Earl Delawarr
FINCH Thomas/13	
FOSTER Richard/12	
FOSTER William/1	
FOWLE Richard*/12	Thomas Fulcher Esq. Liberal
FULCHER Thomas/12	J Biddulph Esq. Liberal
GARDNER John/12	Liberal
GOSLING John/12	
GOURD William/1	
GREEN William/1	
HALE John	
HASTIE Charles Nairn/1	
HEAD William Alston	
HEASMAN Edward Whitley/3	
HEAVER Edward/12	
HISTED John/12	
HOARE John/13	Lord Colchester. Conservative
HOOKER Thomas/12	G S Harcourt Esq. Conservative
HOUNSOME Abraham/12	George Norman Esq. Liberal
HUGGETT Benjamin/13	
HUMMITT James/13	
IRVING Thomas Johnson/12	
KNIGHT Robert/12	
LAMBERT James/12	
LANGRIDGE John/13	

NAME	NAME OF LANDLORD AND/OR OBSERVATIONS
LOWCOCK George	
LYNN James/13	
MAGENS John Dorrien/13	J D Magens Esq. Conservative but friendly to Mr Cavendish
MAGENS Magens Dorrien/13	M D Magens Esq. Conservative but friendly to Mr Cavendish
MARTIN Benjamin/13	
MARTIN Frederick/13	
MARTIN Thomas/12	Earl Burlington
MARTIN William/1	Earl Burlington
MARTIN William/1	J Biddulph Esq. Liberal
MILLS Robert/1	
MITCHELL John/12	
MORPHEW Christopher/1	
NEWMAN Ralph	
OBBARD William/12	Robert Crawford Esq. Conservative
PARROTT William Jackson/12	
PATTENDEN William/12	
PAYNE Robert/13	
PRENTICE John/3	
POCOCK Henry/1	
POLLINGTON Stephen/12	Charity Trustees
RAY John/13	E Cranstone Esq
RIDDLE James/12	E Cranstone Esq
ROBERTS John/13	
ROSE William/12	Earl Delawarr
SANDERS Carew/1	Earl Burlington
SAWYER Charles/12	
SHEARMAN James/12	E Cranstone Esq
SISLEY Richard/1	J Biddulph Esq
SMEED William/3	M D Maggens Esq
SOPER Thomas/12	
SOUTHEY William/12	
STANBRIDGE John/12	Sir Timothy Shelley
STENNING John/1	
SYMONDS Thomas*/12	
TAYLER Henry Thomas/12	
TAYLER Thomas/1	
TAYLER Rev Richard/3	
TURLEY John	
TURNER John/12	
UNDERWOOD John/1	J Biddulph Esq. Liberal
WALLS John/12	J Biddulph Esq
WAGHORN Daniel/1	
WALDER William/12	

NAME	NAME OF LANDLORD AND/OR OBSERVATIONS

WATERS John/12
WELLS William/13
WOOD George/1
WORRELL Jonathan/13
WREN James/12   J Biddulph Esq

EAST GUILDEFORD - 3

OFFEN John/12   Whig
PANKHURST George/12   Whig
      (Broomhill)
WELLS Samuel/2   Whig

EASTHOATHLY - 12

BOURNE John Cane(Hellingly)
BROWN Richard/12
COLGATE Robert/12
LANGDALE Rev Edward/3
MARTIN Matthew/12
PAINE David
RAYNES Edward/12
RICH Henry/12
TESTER Edward/12
VENIS John*/12
WICKERSON John/12
WINTON William/12(Uckfield)

ETCHINGHAM - 15

Rev Dr Tothy and Rev Richard Wetherell have some Influence
in this Parish. Mr Wetherell is an Ultra Tory.

ANDERSON Ambrose/12   Shopkeeper. Independent
AUSTIN Daniel   *Farmer. Sir James Langham Influenced by Mr Wetherell*
DITCH George/2   Farmer. John Ditch. Influenced by Landlord
DUMBRILL John/12   Servant. Dr Tothy. Master
GARNER George sen   *Carpenter. Independent*
HADDON William/12   Measure Maker. Independent
OVERY Cater/23   Farmer. Rev R Wetherell. Influenced by Landlord
PAGE Thomas   *Yeoman. Deaf & Dumb*
RUSSELL Samuel/2   Glazier. Independent
SNEPP John/2   Farmer. Himself. Independent
SNEPP William   *Yeoman. Partly influenced by Mr Snepp.*
SPERLING Charles Robert/23 Gent. Himself. Independent

NAME	NAME OF LANDLORD AND/OR OBSERVATIONS
STANDEN Thomas	*Farmer. Rev R Wetherell. Influenced by his Landlord*
WILLSHER Robert jun/12	Farmer. Rev G Claton. Independent
WOOD Edmund/12	Blacksmith. Independent

EWHURST - 19

Some of the Voters in this Parish are inclined to vote according to the wishes of Mr Tilden Smith of Mountfield. Dr Hewett the Rector is a High Tory.

APPS Edmund/12	Farmer. Himself. Independent
AUSTIN Thomas	*Farmer. Day Esq. Influenced by his Landlord*
BECK William/12	Brewer. Independent
BOOTS Benjamin/12	Wheelwright. Influenced by Mr J Dawes
BURGESS Thomas/12	Butcher. Independent
DAWS Thomas/12	Farmer. Himself. Independent
ELDRIDGE James/12	Shopkeeper. Independent
HEATH Henry/12	Miller. Mr J Richardson. Ind
HENLY Joseph/12	Corn Chandler. Independent
HENLY Thomas/12	Farmer. Independent
HEWETT Rev John Short	*Rector. Independent a Tory*
HILDER Thomas Pain/3	Farmer. Himself. Independent
HYLAND John/12	Innkeeper. Independent
HYLAND William	*Farmer. Independent*
LUCK Richard/12	Farmer. A Doratt Esq. Influenced by his Landlord
REED William/12	Farmer. Himself. Independent
RICHARDSON Thomas/12	Farmer. Independent
SMITH John/12	Yeoman. Independent
SMITH Tilden/12	Farmer. E J Curteis Esq. Influenced by his Landlord

FAIRLIGHT - 7

The Landowners are Lord Liverpool and Messrs Milward & Shadwell the latter Gent has also some indirect influence. Upon the whole not favourable to Mr Cavendish.

BATTY Robert
FIELD James/13
FLOOD Luke Thomas
MARDEN William/12(St Mary in the Castle, Hastings)
THORPE Benjamin/13
THORPE Charles/13
THORPE Christopher/1

NAME	NAME OF LANDLORD AND/OR OBSERVATIONS
	FALMER - 11
ARKCOLL William*/12(Hellingly)	Under Lord Chichester
BARRATT Richard(Brighton)	*Trustees of Roads*
DUNSTALL Wm/12(Brighton)	Independent
FILDER George/12	Lord Chichester's Tenant
GOODDAY Rev John William	*Under Lord Chichester*
MADGWICK William/12	Lord Chichester's Tenant
MOON William/3	Lord Chichester's Tenant
ROGERS Henry/3	Lord Chichester's Tenant
WHITFIELD James/1	Lord Chichester's Tenant
WILKINS Richard/12(Brighton)	Independent
WILLARD William Rogers/12	W C Mabbott's Tenant

FLETCHING - 40

AWCOCK William/12
BANNISTER William/13
BEACON Thomas/3
BENNETT James/12
CARR Henry/12
CAVE William
COATSWORTH David/13
DAVIES Lieut Col Francis John/12
DAVIES Warburton/12
DIPLOCK William
DURRANT Stephen/13
FLEET Benjamin/12
FRIEND David/12
FULLER James
GAUNT Rev Charles
GILBERT Edward/3
GILBERT Daniel/3
GILBERT William/12
GOORD William/12
HEMSLEY George/12
KEMBER John/13
KENWARD James/12
NOAKES John/12
OSBORN James/12
OSBORN Thomas/13
PARKER William
POLLARD Robert/12
PRATT John/12
ROGERS Daniel/12
STEVENSON George/12

NAME	NAME OF LANDLORD AND/OR OBSERVATIONS

TOMSETT John/12
TOMSETT Thomas/12
TURNER George*/12
URIDGE Isaac/12
VINALL William/12
WHEELER William/12
WILSON Sir Thomas Maryon, bart/3
WOOD Charles
WOOLETT Thomas
YOUNG Richard/13

FOLKINGTON - 6

DENNES Thomas/13	Influenced by William Harrison Esq
HARRISON William/13	A Tory
KELSON Rev Henry/13	A Tory. Presented to his Living by late Duchess of Dorset
PAGDEN John/13	Tenant of William Harrison Esq
SEARLE Stephen/13	Tenant of William Harrison Esq
TUTT Richard/13	Influenced by William Harrison Esq

FRAMFIELD - 39

ADAMS John/12
BANKS Joseph/12
BARTON William/12
BERWICK Edward/13   Tenant of Rev P Woodward
BONNEY George/12
BROWN Henry/12
BURTON Benjamin
BURTON William
CORNWELL Stephen sen/12
CORNWELL Stephen jun
DONOVAN A(Framfield & East
        Grinstead)
ELLMAN John   *Dead*
GUY Samuel/12
HEMSLEY John*/13
HELMSLEY Samuel/12
HILLS John/12
HOARE Rev Henry/3
HOMEWOOD John jun/12
HUGHES William/12
KENWARD William/12
LEDNER Driver William/12
MARCHANT Charles/12
MARTIN William/12

```
NAME                              NAME OF LANDLORD AND/OR OBSERVATIONS
MORRIS Anthony/3                  Tenant of Lord Gage
NEWNHAM Henry/12
NEWNHAM Robert/12
PACKHAM Thomas/13
PAGE John/12
PETERS James/12
RASON William/1(Willingdon)Tenant of Earl Burlington
RELF William/13                   Reeve to Earl Delawarr
SMITH John/3
SMITH John/13(Wadhurst)
STAPLEY Robert*/13                Tenant to the Ellman family
STARR Thomas/12
STEPHENS John/12
THOMSON Philip/12
WALLER Samuel/12                  Influenced by the Rev P Woodward
WALLIS Thomas/3
```

FRANT - 29

Those marked with a + are chiefly Tenants or Tradespeople
of the Earl of Abergavenny and are at present influenced by
Mr Rowland, His Lordship's Steward.
The Earl himself it is understood from Age and infirmity
does not interfere.
Those marked thus = are Tenants or Tradespeople to the Earl
Camden and likely to vote as he wishes.
Stephen Jones - Fairbrother Powell & Cheesman had
originally promised to vote for Cavendish and Curteis but
were subsequently induced by Lord Camden's Steward two of
them not to vote at all and two of them to split with
Darby.
Those not marked are supposed to be independent men.

```
BLACKWELL George+/12
BUDGEN William
BYE Colonel John
CARD John+/12
CARR John+/12
CAVIE William+/12
CHEESMAN Charles=/13
CLARKE William=/12
FAIRBROTHER Henry=
FIELD Edward+/12
FIELD William+/12
FULLJAMES Richard+/12
HATTON Captain Villiers Francis
```

34

NAME	NAME OF LANDLORD AND/OR OBSERVATIONS

HICKMOTT Timothy+
HOMEWOOD William+/12
JACOB Adam
JEFFERY William/12
JONES Richard sen/12
JONES Stephen=
KINE Edward/2
MACFARLANE Major James
MERIET Captain George Lewis
MOON Thomas/12
POWELL James/13
ROGERS Robert/12
ROPER William/3
ROWLAND Daniel*/12
STARTIN George/12
WICKENS Obid/12

FRISTON - 1

SCRASE William/13 — Tenant to Lord Liverpool

FULKING - 5

HOWELL Charles/12 — Tenant of Mrs Baker, Portland Place, London
MARCHANT William/12 — Independent
MOON Humphrey/12 — Independent
STEVENS James/12 — Independent
STREVENS James/12 — Independent

GLYNDE - 5

ELLMAN John jun — *General Trevor's Tenant*
MORLEY John/12
ROSE Rev William/13 — Under General Trevor's influence and also Lord Abergavenny
TREVOR Major General the Hon Henry Otway/1
WISDOM Thomas/1 — General Trevor's Tenant

GUESTLING - 11

The Landowners are Lord Liverpool, Sir William Ashburnham and Mr Briscoe. Mr Shadwell has a little indirect influence.

ASHBURNHAM Rev J(Guestling & Pevensey)
ASHBURNHAM Sir William, bart/12
BENFIELD Nathaniel/2
BOURNE John/12

NAME	NAME OF LANDLORD AND/OR OBSERVATIONS

CLOKE Moses/12
CLOKE William/12
GILFIN John
GILFIN William/13
HARMAN George/12
HAY Robert Benjamin
OVERY Robert/12

HAILSHAM - 33

BAKER James Bray/13
BAKER Walter/12
BARNETT John/13   George Weller
BREADS Henry/12(All Saints, Lewes)
BURFIELD Thomas/12
CAREY John Nicholas/12
CLARE John Gibson*/12
ELMES Edwin/2
GEERING Thomas/12
GOLDSMITH William/12
GURNETT Caleb/2
HILDER Henry
HODE James
JAMES Samuel/12
KENWARD Robert/12
LONG William/12
LONGLEY Jeremiah/12
MYNN John/12
OSBORNE Bartholomew/12
PAGDEN Peter/13
PEIRCE Thomas/12   Gillon Esq
RICKMAN Nathaniel/12(Herstmonceux)
SAMPSON Richard King/12
SINNOCK Samuel
SLYE William/3
STAFFORD William Whitmore/13
STREDWICK Thomas/13
TERRY Samuel/12
VERELL William/12   J Luxford Esq
WATERS Henry Harcourt
WELCH Rev Thomas Robinson/3
WELLER George/13
WELLER John/12
WINSER James/12

NAME	NAME OF LANDLORD AND/OR OBSERVATIONS

HAMSEY - 10

AYLWIN James(Chiddingly)	T Partington Esq. Rejected
GUY Nathaniel/12	Sir C M Burrell
HOLMAN Samuel/12	Sir G Shiffner. Influenced by Mr Jenner
KELL Smith Thomas/13	Lord Liverpool
LASHMAR James/12	Sir Timothy Shelley
PARTINGTON Thomas*/1	Earl Burlington
SHIFFNER Sir George,bart/13	Palace
SHIFFNER Rev George/13	Palace
URIDGE Henry/12	Independent
VERRALL Richard	*Dead*

HANGLETON - 1

HARDWICK John/3(Portslade)	Tenant of Lord Delawarr

HARTFIELD - 18

ATHERFOLD Henry	*Earl Delawarr*
BRIDGER James/1	
BROOKER Ambrose/3	Earl Delawarr
EDWARDS Robert/3	Earl Delawarr
GREENLAND George Thomas	
GASSON Richard/12	Mrs Whatley
HENNIKER Hon Major Jacob/1	
HILL John/1	A E Fuller Esq. Friendly to Mr Cavendish
HOOKER John/12	Lord Delawarr
JACKSON Henry Humphrey/13	
JOWETT Rev John/13	
KENWARD William/12	M D Magens Esq
MAITLAND Lieut Gen Fredk/3	
MARCHANT Charles/12	
NEWTON John sen/1	
PHILCOX George/1	Earl Delawarr
RICHARDS Thomas/3	
STEER William/12	

HASTINGS - ALL SAINTS - 27

The Hastings Voters as a body are independent. Mr Shadwell has much influence as any <u>one</u> Person. Mr Milward too has influence but neither are likely to use it and certainly not against Mr Cavendish. This remark applies to All Saints, St Clements and St Mary in the Castle.

BANKS Benjamin/12(St Clement)

BEVINS John/13
BURCHATT Edward/12
COUSSENS Henry/12(St Clement)
COUSSENS John/12
ELPHICK John*/12
FENNER David/3
HALL William/12
HANNAY Joseph/12
HARMAN Richard/12
HARVEY Anthony sen/12
HUTCHINSON T Curtis/12(St Mary in the Castle)
JONES George Clarke*/12(St Clement)
KENT Philip/12(St Mary in the Castle)
MILLS John/12
NORMAN William/12(Hellingly)
NORTH Frederick(St Clement)
RIDLEY William*/12
SHADWELL William Lucas(Fairlight)
TICHBON Thomas/1
TUTT George sen/12
WEBB John*/12
WHITE Thomas/12
WHITING Thomas/12
WINGFIELD George/12(St Mary in the Castle)
WINTER James/12
WOOD Joseph/12(St Clement)

HASTINGS - ST CLEMENT - 52
See remarks as for Hastings All Saints.

ADAMS John/12
AMOORE William/12
BAYLEY William/12
BREEDS James/12(St Mary in the Castle)
BREEDS Thomas/12
BREEDS Thomas James/2
BRISCO Wastel sen/12(Ore)
BROWNE Joseph/12(St Mary in the Castle)
CHAPMAN William*/12
DANIEL Thomas/3
DUKE Samuel
EATON John/12(St Mary in the Castle)
EDWARDS William/12
EMARY Francis*/12
FOORD John/12

NAME	NAME OF LANDLORD AND/OR OBSERVATIONS

FOSTER Thomas*/12(St Mary in the Castle)
GEORGE George/12(All Saints)
HARMAN Benjamin*/12
HART James
HINKLEY John*/12(All Saints)
HINKLEY Robert/12
HUTCHINSON Thomas/12
JACKSON George/12(All Saints)
KELLAND Matthew/12(St Mary in the Castle)
MANNINGTON John/12
MIDDLEMAS Richard/12(Battle)
MILWARD Edward
PAYNE William/12(St Mary in the Castle)
PHILLIPS John jun/12(St Mary in the Castle)
PHILLIPS John sen(St Mary in the Castle)
ROBINSON George sen*/12
RUSSELL John/12
SCRIVENS William/1(Guestling)
SHAW William/12(Bexhill)
SHORTER John Goldsworthy/12
SHORTER John Goldsworthy jun(All Saints)
SINNOCK Thomas/12
SMITH Francis/12(Catsfield)
SMITH John/12(St Mary in the Castle)
SMITH John/12(Winchelsea)
STANDEN Benjamin/12(St Mary in the Castle)
STONESTREET Rev G S G(St Mary in the Castle)
STRICKLAND George*/2
THORPE William
TICEHURST Frederick/3(Battle)
TYHURST Edward/12
WELLERD William/12
WHEELER John/12
WILLIAMS John sen/12
WILLIAMS John jun/12
WIMBLE N Harrison/12(St Mary in the Castle)
WOOD William/12

HASTINGS - ST LEONARD - 14

BURTON James
CORK John/12(St Clement)
FARNCOMBE Edward/12
HOMAN B/12(St Leonards & St Mary Magdalen)
HOMAN James/12(St Mary Magdalen)
LEAVE Tom/13

NAME	NAME OF LANDLORD AND/OR OBSERVATIONS

MADDEN Rd. Rt.(St Mary Magdalen)
MILSTED Stephen/12(St Mary Magdalen)
OVERY Charles
PUTLAND Stephen/12(St Mary Magdalen)
SCOTT George/12(St Mary Magdalen)
TOWNER Thomas/12(St Mary Magdalen)
WAGHORN Edward(Hooe)
WOODS Joseph

> Those marked thus + have no Votes. Mr Cavendish's Agent
> did not raise an(sic) question before the revising
> Barrister because he knew they were friendly to Mr Cav-
> endish he did not however press them to vote but on the
> contrary in persuance of the instructions from Mr Cav-
> endish's central Committee told them they had not legal
> votes and left them to act on their own Responsibility, the
> others are independent the little there is in the Parish
> (little enough it is) is in Mr Burton who would have voted
> for Mr Cavendish the last Election but arrived too late.

{The above note is inserted in this position but no names are
thus marked}

HASTINGS - ST MARY IN THE CASTLE - 42
See remarks as for Hastings All Saints.

AUSTIN John/1(St Clement)
BAYLEY John jun/12
BEALE Joseph/12
BECK Henry/12(Eastbourne)
BREEDS Boykett/2(Holy Trinity)
BRYANT John/12(St Clement)
CAMAC W/12(St Mary in the Castle & Westfield)
CHANDLER Richard
CLEMENT George
CROWHURST Thomas/12(Rye)
DAY Peter/12(All Saints)
DE VANDES Alexander(Fairlight)
DUKE William/12(Battle)
EMARY James/12
EMARY Thomas Reeve/12
FURNER Jesse Ades/12
GALLOP George/12
GLANDFIELD John George

NAME	NAME OF LANDLORD AND/OR OBSERVATIONS

HAYWARD John/12
HARMAN James/1(Rye)
HONISS Edward(St Mary Magdalen)
HONISS William Henry(St Mary Magdalen)
LONGLEY William/12(St Clement)
MURRAY John/23
NASH Richard/12
PHILLIPS James/12
POMPHREY Joshua Bossom(Bexhill)
REED Jonathan/12(Hollington)
RIDLEY William/12
RISBY James/13
ROBINSON George jun/12
SMITH Jno
STANDEN Thomas*/12
STEEVENS Edward
THWAITES George/12
THWAITES Jno Dungate/12(St Clement)
TREE Benjamin*/1
WAGHORN Mercer/12(Hooe)
WILLIAMSON John Wilkins/13
WINGFIELD Henry/12(St Clement)
WINTER William*/12
WOODHAMS Jno Latter/12(St Clement)

HASTINGS - ST MARY MAGDALEN - 4

Here Mr Wood of Lewes may influence one and Sir J G Thomas
the Trustee of the Eversfield Estate another.

DEUDNEY Robert/12
ELDRIDGE William/23
HYLAND George/12
JEFFERIES Joseph/2

HASTINGS - HOLY TRINITY - 1

Government owns the greater part of the Grounds in this
Parish which is built upon but it being within the limits
of the Borough occupants do not vote for the County.
Thorne is under no influence.

THORNE Thomas/12(St Mary Magdalen)

NAME	NAME OF LANDLORD AND/OR OBSERVATIONS

HEATHFIELD - 59

Mr Darby has some influence in this Parish which he used to
his utmost as did also the Vicar the Rev J Young,
Sir Charles Blunt and Mr Fuller of Brightling have
influence but neither of them used it

NAME	NAME OF LANDLORD AND/OR OBSERVATIONS
ASHDOWN James	*Farmer. Himself. Independent*
BAKER John jun/3	Farmer. Sir C Blunt. Agt M C on Account of Water Scott assessment
BAKER John sen/3	Farmer. Sir C Blunt. Agt M C on Account of Water Scott assessment
BAKER Samuel/13	Farmer. Himself. Independent
BALCOMB John	*Miller. Independent*
BARROW William/12	Farmer. late Chambers. Ind
BARTON Thomas/3	Nurseryman. Himself & Sir C Blunt. Influenced by his Customers
BRYANT Benjamin*/12	Shopkeeper. Independent
BURTON Mark/13	Farmer. Himself. Independent
CHRISMAS George/3	Farmer. Influenced by Mr Darby
CHRISMAS Thomas	*Farmer. Influenced by Mr Darby*
COLLINGS Joseph/3	Farmer & Higler. Influenced by Mr Darby
DALLAWAY Samuel/3	Miller. Influenced by Mr Darby
DRAY William/3	Collar Maker. Influenced by Mr Darby
ERREY William/12	Farmer. Independent
FEATHERSTONE John/12	Farmer. Independent
FULLER George/3	Esquire. J Fuller Esq. Ind (a Tory)
GOBLE Theophilus/3	Shopkeeper. Influenced by Mr Darby
HAFFENDEN George/13	Wheelwright. Independent
HAFFENDEN James jun/12	Farmer. Independent
HAFFENDEN James sen/12	Farmer. Independent
HAFFENDEN Richard/12	Farmer. Independent
HAFFENDEN Robert/12	Farmer. Mr Jno Woodward. Ind
HAFFENDEN Titus/12	Farmer. J Fuller Esq. Independent
HARMER Henry/3	Farmer. J P Durrant. Influenced by his Landlord
HARMER Jonathan/12	Stonemason. Independent
HARMER Joseph/1	Farmer. Independent
HAYWARD Michael/12	Farmer. Independent
HICKS Thomas/3	Farmer. Garland Esq. Independent
HOBDEN John/2	Farmer. Goring Esq. Independent
HOWELL John/12	Innkeeper. Himself. Independent
HUGGETT James/12	Farmer. Goring Esq. Independent
HUGGETT John/12	Farmer. J Fuller Esq. Independent

NAME	NAME OF LANDLORD AND/OR OBSERVATIONS
HUNT John/3	Common Carrier. J Fuller Esq & Miles Esq. Influenced by Mr Darby
KEMP Henry/3	Farmer & Bailiff. Influenced by Mr Darby
KEMP Peter/3	Shopkeeper. Influenced by Mr Darby
KNIGHT Thomas jun/1	Miller. Independent
LONGLEY Charles/12	Farmer. Sir C Blunt. Independent
MEPHAM Thomas/12	Farmer. Independent
MEPHAM Thomas Miller/12	Miller. Independent
OVERY William/12	Farmer. R Overy. Independent
OXLEY William jun/12	Farmer. Goring Esq. Independent
PAINE William/13	Farmer. Independent
PETTIT John/3	Farmer. Independent
PETTIT Samuel/3	Farmer. Independent
PRESS Rev J/3(Heathfield & Burwash)	Dissenting Minister an Hippocrite
RELF James/12	Farmer. Sir C Blunt. Independent
ROADES Thomas/1	Farmer. Himself. Independent
SKINNER William/12	Farmer & Miller. Sir C Blunt. Ind
STONE William/13	Surgeon. Independent
THOMSON Jonathan Smith/12	Farmer & Shopkeeper. Independent
THOMSON Samuel/12	Yeoman. Independent
UPFIELD William/1	Glazier. Independent
VALENTINE John/3	Shoemaker. Influenced by Mr Darby
WATERS Stephen/13	Farmer. Independent
WELLER John	*Farmer. J A Dalrymple Esq. Ind*
WHITE Samuel/13	Farmer. J Fuller Esq. Independent
WINCHESTER Henry/12	Carpenter. Independent
YOUNG Rev James/3	Vicar. Independent a Tory

HEIGHTON - 3

CORNER William/12	Uninfluenced
GEERE William/12	Uninfluenced
WOOLGAR George/12	Uninfluenced

HELLINGLY - 35

ASHDOWN Daniel/23	
BEENY William/12	
BENNETT John/12	
BISHOP James/12	
BLUNDEN John*/12	
BUTLER William	*Thomas Calverly Esq*
CHAPMAN Edward/3	
CLAPSON George/12	
CLAPSON John*/2	

NAME	NAME OF LANDLORD AND/OR OBSERVATIONS
COMBER Joseph/12	
COOMBE Thomas*/3	
DAWES Thomas	
DUNK James/12	
DUNK Thomas/12	
FREEMAN George/12	Mr Edward Hart
GOODWIN Thomas/12	
GOSDEN John/12	Mrs Mason
HOLMAN Thomas/12	
HUMPHREY David/12	
KENNARD Stephen/12	
MARTIN Thomas sen*/12	
MARTIN Thomas jun/12	J Fuller Esq
MILLER William/12	
MORRIS Samuel	
NOAKES Robert/12	Calverly Esq
OLIVE Rev John/3	
PAGE Richard/12	J Smith Esq
PARRIS John	
PATTENDEN John/3	J Wynn Esq
PITCHER Robert/12	
RICKMAN David/12	Lord Chichester
RUSSELL William/12	
TERRY Alfred/1	Mr John Clapson
THORPE William/12	
WELLER William/12	Mr King

HERSTMONCEUX - 36

ALLFREE William/12	
ARKCOLL Thomas/12	
BARNARD Ned/12	
BEENY Edward/2	
BROOK James/12	
COLMAN James/12	
COSHAM Thomas Shadwell	
CROUCH William/12	
DANN David/12(Wartling)	
DEWDNEY C/12(Herstmonceux & Pevensey)	
EVERESTS James jun/12	
EVERESTS James sen/12	
GORHAM Beadle/12	
GORRINGE James	*J Day Esq*
HONNISETT William/12	
MARTIN Henry/12	Gillon Esq
MILLER Thomas/12	Gillon Esq

NAME	NAME OF LANDLORD AND/OR OBSERVATIONS
NOAKES Samuel/12	Gillon Esq
NOAKES Samuel/12(Burwash)	
PURSGLOVE Richard/2	
PURSGLOVE Robert/12	Lord Ashburnham
SAMPSON Thomas S/12	
SMITH Isaac/12	
SMITH Jesse/12	T S Sampson
SMITH Richard/12(Wartling)	
STONE Peter	
STUBBERFIELD John/12	
TAYLOR Edward/12	Gillon Esq
VINALL Thomas/2	
VINE Thomas Pinton/12	Sir Jno Fagg
WAGNER George Henry M/3	
WINCHESTER Joseph/12	
WINCHESTER Richard/12	
WRATTEN David/2(Hailsham)	
WRATTEN Isaac/12	
YOUNG James/12	Gillon Esq

HOLLINGTON - 6

Sir Charles Lamb and Mr J C Pelham have the chief Influence here.

FARNCOMB William
LAMB Sir Charles Montolieu, bart
MAPLESDEN Richard*/12
POCOCK William/12
STARR Thomas/3
WEST John/12

HOOE - 8

BLACKMAN Benjamin/23	Tenant of Lord Ashburnham's
BLACKMAN Edward/12(Wartling)	Independent
COLEMAN John/3	Tenant of J Fuller Esq
FOX Stephen/12	Tenant of Mr Sampson Battle & Mr Tamworth Hastings
HENBREY Robert/12	Independent
LEWIS William/12	Tenant of John Fuller Esq
LOCK John/12	Workman of and under influence of Mr Fox
MITTEN Joseph/3	Tenant of Edward Pennyfather of Dublin

NAME	NAME OF LANDLORD AND/OR OBSERVATIONS

HORSTED KEYNES - 19

AUSTEN Rev William
ARNOLD Thomas*/12
ARNOLD William/12
AWCOCK George/12
BURT Richard/12
BURTENSHAW John/12
BRIGDEN James/12
CHATFIELD Nicholas/12
COMBER John/12
FISHER Henry(Brighton)
HOLMAN Thomas/12
JENNER Robert/12
MARTEN Thomas*/12
OBBARD George/12
ROSER John/12
ROSER Richard/12
STONE John/12
VERRALL George
WARNETT William/12

HOVE - 16

The voters in this Parish are all Independent.

ADAMS Charles Marsh
BOWELL Joseph/12(Brighton)
BUSBY Charles Augustin/12(Hove & Brighton)
BUTCHER Rev Edward Robert*/13(Portslade)
DICKENS Charles Scrase jun/13(West Blatchington)
EVERARD Rev Edward D D/1
HILL George Philcox/13(Brighton)
HOWELL Charles/12(Brighton)
LAMBERT William
MALLESON Jno Philip/12(Brighton)
MILLS James/12
SARGENT Henry*/12(Brighton)
STEPHENS George/12(Hove & Brighton)
STRANGE John/13
VALLANCE John
WIGNEY William/12(Brighton)

HURSTPIERPOINT - 25

BORRER Nathaniel/13
CAMPION William John/13
CHANDLER William/13

46

NAME	NAME OF LANDLORD AND/OR OBSERVATIONS

CROSKEY Thomas Page/13
DAVEY Richard
ELLIS William
EDWARDS James
GOODMAN Samuel/13(Hurstpierpoint & Brighton)
HIDER Henry/12
HOLMAN Henry
LEMPRIER John Sturch/12
MARCHANT John/12
MARSHALL James/13
MARSHALL William(Bolney)
MITCHELL James*/12
MITCHELL John/13(Cliffe,Lewes)
MITTEN William/3
NYE Richard
TUFNELL Rev John Charles F/3(Bolney)
UWINS Thomas/12
WEBBER George*/12
WEEKES Richard jun/13
WEEKES Richard/13
WELLS Peter/12
WICKHAM Jesse/13

ICKLESHAM - 17

NAME	NAME OF LANDLORD AND/OR OBSERVATIONS
AMOS Daniel/12	Tennant(sic) to Mr Briscoe
BEAL John/1	Whig
BENFIELD Joel/12(Winchelsea)	Tenant to D Dawes Esq
CAREY Jacob/12	Whig
CAREY Lewis/12	Whig
CAREY Thomas/12	Whig
CRASSINGHAM Richard/12	Whig
FARNCOMB Henry/12(St Mary in the Castle,Hastings)	Whig
HARMAN John	*Defunct*
HOAD Christopher/12 (Guestling)	Whig. Tenant to Tory Landlord
HOAD John/12	Whig
MARTIN Edward/12	Whig
MONK John*/13	Whig
RICHARDS Rev Thomas*/13	Tory says he will always support Mr Cavendish but is not to be depended upon
SIMMONDS John/12	Whig
VENIS Isaac/12	Whig
WILSON James/12(Winchelsea)	Whig

NAME	NAME OF LANDLORD AND/OR OBSERVATIONS

IDEN - 5

BOWLES Jeffery/2	Whig
HARRISON Thomas	*Tory*
LAMB Rev George Augustus/3	Tory
OLIVER John/2	Whig
TURK John/12	Whig

IFORD - 3

DONALD Rev Matthewman	*Under Mr Hurley's Influence*
Hodgson	
HURLY Henry	*Banker, Lewes*
RIDGE Joseph/12	Liberal

ISFIELD - 5

ATREE Richard	
DONOVAN James	*Dead*
HUNTLEY George/12	
HEAVER Edward/12	
MANNINGTON Peter*/12	

JEVINGTON - 3

ADE Henry/12	Tenant of Earl of B
NOAKES Thomas/12	Tenant of Capt Bligh
REEDS Samuel/12	Tenant of Capt Warrenford

KEYMER - 6

FORD Thomas Welfare/12
JENNER Philip/12
MARTEN Henry/12
MARTEN John
NORMAN William/12
PIERCE Richard/12

KINGSTON - 1

WISE Thomas/12	Under influence of Mr J Marten, Rodmell

LAMBERHURST - 15

Those not marked are supposed to be independent men. Those marked + are Tenants or Tradespeople of Lord Camden.

BALLARD Isaac/12	Independent
BARTON Thomas/12	
BLACKMAN John/12(Ticehurst)	
BOORMAN James/12	

NAME	NAME OF LANDLORD AND/OR OBSERVATIONS

CRIPPS John/12
CUTBEARTH John/12
GOLDSTON William
HICKMOTT John/12
HUSSEY Edward/13
LANSDELL Thomas/12
LASHMAR John Lulham/3   Tory
MORLAND William Alexander
NOAKES John/12
PRICKETT Charles   *The 2 Pricketts had partly promised to*
PRICKETT Thomas   *vote for the Whig Candidates but it is*
                             understood were somewhat influenced by
                             their Landlord Sir J Filmer an Ultra
                             and therefore did not vote.

LAUGHTON - 8

BARROW Joseph/12
SCRACE Edward*/12   Earl of Chichester
SHOOSMITH John/12   Earl of Chichester
SHOOSMITH Joseph/12   Earl of Chichester
STARNES Stephen/12   Earl of Chichester
STARNES Thomas/1   Earl of Chichester's Reeve
WHAPHAM William/12   Earl of Chichester
WOOD Rowland/12   Earl of Chichester

LEWES - ALL SAINTS - 70

ADAMS George/12
ADAMS John/12
ATTWOOD Wiliiam(sic)/12
BARBER Edward/12(St John)
BEARD Edward/12(St John)
BLACKMAN Henry/12(St John)
BLAKER Edgar(St John)
BLAKER John jun(St John)
BLAKER John sen/12(St Michael)
BOLLEN Thomas/12(Brighton)
BOORE Charles/12(St John)
BROWNE Henry/12
BRYANT Thomas/12
CAREY John/12(St Michael)
CROSSKEY William/12(Ditcheling)
EGLES Gabriel jun(Brighton)
EGLES Gabriel sen*/1(Southmalling)
FISHER Thomas/12
FULLER William

NAME	NAME OF LANDLORD AND/OR OBSERVATIONS

GELL F H*/1(Eastbourne, St John & Chailey)
GIBBS James/13(St John)
GOSLING Jesse/13
GRIFFITHS John Henry Thomas/13(Warbleton)
HAMMOND Nathan/12
HARMAN George/12
HICK W F (Maresfield & Lindfield)
HICKS Thomas*/13
HOPER George/13(Crowhurst)
HOPER John sen/13(Beddingham)
HOTHER Charles/12(All Saints & Cliffe)
HOTHER George/13
HOTHER John
INSKIP George/13(Ringmer)   Influenced by Messrs Hoper
INSKIP John/3(St John)   Influenced by Messrs Hoper
ISTED Edmund/1
JOHNSTON T jun/13(Cliffe & Laughton)
KING Joseph/12
LAMBE Richard(Cliffe)
LAMBE William/13(All SaintsInfluenced by Messrs Hoper
        & Cliffe)
LEE Frederick William/12(St Michael)
LOWER Reuben William/12(St John)
MADGWICK John Chatfield/12
MADGWICK Thomas/12(Cliffe)
MADGWICK William sen/12(Southmalling)
MANNINGTON William/12(Ripe)
MARSH Thomas/12(St John)
MARTEN Thomas/12
MORRIS Benjamin/3(Ringmer)
NEWMAN William/13(Brighton)
PARSONS Latter*/1
PENFORD James/12
PORTER John*/1(St Michael)
RICKMAN John*/12(All Saints & Cliffe)
ROBINSON Thomas/12(Southmalling)
STEDMAN James/12
SMITH John(Burwash)
SMITH William/12(St John)
SMITH William(Southover)
TUGWELL Richard/12(Glynde)
TURNER Richard/13(Brighton)
VALENTINE Rev C Porteus/12(Chailey)
VERRALL Plumer/12
WATTS George/12

NAME	NAME OF LANDLORD AND/OR OBSERVATIONS

WESTON E (All Saints,Lewes & Hastings)
WHITFELD Thomas/13
WILLE Charles sen/12
WIMBLE Nehemiah/12
WOOD John Marten/12(Barcombe)
WOOD Thomas/12(Cliffe)
WOOLLGAR John Webb(Cliffe) Mr Curteis's Agent

LEWES - CASTLE PRECINCT - 3

LANGFORD Benjamin Cooper/12(St John)
LANGFORD John/12(St John)
SHELLEY John/12(Chailey & St Michael)

Brothers to Lord Burlington's Tenants. Independent

LEWES - CLIFFE - 43

BROWN Abraham/12
BUNTING Charles/12
CARLETON Edward Augustus*/1(Newhaven)
CLEAR Henry/12(Brighton)
DAVIES James/12(Ringmer)
EVERSHED Thomas/12(St John)
FARNES John sen/12
FARNES John jun/12
FREEMAN John/12
GATES James/12(Mayfield)
GARNHAM Barnhard/12
GEERING John/12
GEST Richard/12(All Saints)
GOODYER Richard/12(Cliffe) Disqualified
GREEN Henry/12
GROVER James/12(Southmalling)Influenced by J Hillman
GROVER John/13   Influenced by J Hillman
GROVER Simon
HARVEY Daniel/1
HARVEY John/12(All Saints)
HICKS George/12
HILLMAN Henry/3
HILLMAN John/13
HOEY George Beard/13
HOEY George/13
KING Thomas/12(Ringmer)
LENEY Isaac/12
LENEY Samuel/13
MARTIN Richard/12

NAME	NAME OF LANDLORD AND/OR OBSERVATIONS
MORRIS Arthur/12(Brighton)	
MORRIS Ebenezer/3	
NUTLEY Edward/12	
NUTLEY Caleb/12	
PECKHAM George*/12	
PORTER Richard/12(St John)	
RUSBRIDGE Benjamin/12	Influenced by Mr Newton
RUSBRIDGE Charles/12	Influenced by Mr Newton
RUSBRIDGE William/12	Influenced by Mr Newton
SIMMONS William	
VENUS John/12	
VERRALL Alexander/23	
WILLE Charles jun/12(Southmalling)	
WILLE George	

LEWES - ST ANNE - 15

BARCHARD Francis/13	A Tory
BOXALL John/3	A Tory
COMBER Benjamin/13	A Tory
(All Saints)	
FOLD John sen/13	A Tory
GARNHAM Stephen(Brighton)	*Would not vote*
GEAR Robert/13	A Tory
GOLDFINCH Henry/3(Arlington)	A Tory
LANGRIDGE William/12	Liberal
LANGRIDGE Wm Balcombe/12	Liberal. Clerk of the Peace
MOLINEUX George	*Bank*
RICHARDSON Thos/13(Barcombe)	A Tory
RIDGE Benjamin/12(Street)	Liberal
WESTON John/12(Mayfield)	Liberal
WILLIAMS Rev C K/13	A Tory
(Hamsey & St Michael)	
WINTER John/3	A Tory under Mr Gear's influence

LEWES - ST JOHN - 42

ATWOOD William/3(Cliffe)	A Tory his Majesty's Silversmith
BATES John/12(All Saints)	Liberal
BECKETT John/12	Liberal
BOORE Edward/12	Liberal
BOORE Frederick/13	Liberal
BRIDGER Wm/12(All Saints)	Liberal
BROWN William/12	Liberal
BUTLAND James/13	Tory
COOPER William/13	Lord Liverpool's Tenant and influenced by him
CORNER Wm/12(All Saints)	Liberal

NAME	NAME OF LANDLORD AND/OR OBSERVATIONS
COWPER John	*County Surveyor*
CRUTTENDEN William	*Dead*
DEADMAN William/13	Sir James Scarlett's Tenant and influenced by him
DUDENEY John/12	Liberal. Dissenting Minister
DUPLOCK Stephen/12 (All Saints)	Liberal
ELLMAN John/13(Keymer)	Under General Trevor's influence
FENNELL James/13	A Tory under influence of Mr Latter Parsons
FIEST Richard/12(All Saints)	Liberal
FIGG William/13(E.Grinstead)	Under Mr Hoper's Influence
FLINT Samuel/12(Cliffe & Waldron)	Liberal
FRANCIS Philip/12	Liberal
HACKMAN George/12	Liberal. Sir George Shiffner's Tenant
HAMLIN John/12(Southmalling)	Liberal
HARMAN Sargent/13	A Tory
HART George Edward/12 (Hellingly)	Liberal
HOLDEN Stephen/12(Cuckfield)	Liberal
INSOLL Richard(Southover)	*Landlord of Starr Inn would not vote*
KNIGHT William/12	Liberal
LEE Warren/12(St. Michael)	Liberal
MAXFIELD Joseph*/12	Liberal
PHILLIPS James/23(All Saints)	A man of no principle
POTTER Isaac/12	Liberal
POTTER Peter/12	Liberal
ROBINSON George/12	Liberal
ROOKE John/12	Liberal
RUSBRIDGE Stephen/13	Under Mr Croft's Influence
SHORT Henry/12	Liberal
STEPHENS Charles/13	A Tory
TOURLE Thomas	*A Tory*
WALLER James/13	A Tory
WATTS William/12	Liberal
WRIGHT William/12	Liberal

ST. MICHAEL - 30

ALDERTON Richard/12	Liberal
BAILEY George sen/12	Liberal
BULL Peter/12(St John)	Liberal
CARTER William/12	Liberal. Mr Cavendish's Agent
COOPER Thomas*/1	Under Mr Hurley's Influence
DAVEY William	*Banker*

NAME	NAME OF LANDLORD AND/OR OBSERVATIONS
DICKER Thomas(St Ann & Brighton	*Liberal*
GOLDSMITH Edward/12(Brighton)	A Tory under J.C. Pelham's Influence
GRANTHAM George sen(StAnn)	*Liberal. Distributor of Stamps*
GRANTHAM George jun/12 (Southover & Lindfield)	Liberal
HAMMOND James/12	Liberal
HOBDEN John/12(All Saints)	Removed
HOLMDEN George	*Liberal*
HUGGETT John/12(Southover)	Liberal
KELL Christopher/3 (Fletching& Mayfield)	Mr Darby's Agent
LEONARD James(All Saints)	*Liberal but prevented from voting by Mr Lowdell*
LOWDELL Stephen/13 (StMichael & All Saints)	a man of no principle
MANTELL Gideon/12 (St Michael & St John)	Surgeon. Liberal
NEAL Edwin/13(St John)	A Tory. His Majesty's Shoemaker
NEAL Robert/23	A Tory voted by mistake but promised all three
PARKER Wm/12(All Saints)	Liberal
POLLARD John(Southover)	*Excise Officer*
SMART William/12	Liberal
SMART Samuel Hide/12	Liberal
VERRAL Edward/3(Chiddingly)	Mr Darby's Agent
VERRALL William jun/12 (Southover)	Liberal
WATERS John(Warbleton)	*would not promise*
WHITEMAN Thas/13(All Saints)	a Tory his Majesty's Tailor
WILLARD Richard/12	Liberal
WINDUS Arthur E B/13(St John)	Liberal

SOUTHMALLING - 15

BERRY James jun/12(All Saints)	
BERRY Thomas/12(Cliffe)	
CAMPION Henry/13	
CHATFIELD Thomas(All Saints)	
CROFTS Rev P Guerin/3(St John)	
ELLMAN Thomas(Glynde)	*General Trevor's Tenant*
GRANTHAM Stephen/13	Lord Liverpool's Steward
HILLMAN Samuel/13(St John)	
MORRIS Thomas*/13	Lord Gage's Tenant
PETTET Thomas sen/12	
PETTET Thomas jun	

NAME	NAME OF LANDLORD AND/OR OBSERVATIONS
PHILCOX Moses/13	
RIDGE William/12	Tenant to Sir C M Burrell
ROBINSON Samuel/12	
SAUNDERS John/12	

SOUTHOVER - 21

BAKER James/13	A Tory
CHEALE Charles/12	Liberal
CRUTTENDEN Thomas/12	Liberal
FAIRHALL John/12	Liberal
FORD William/12	Liberal
GOLDSMITH John/3	Conscientious Tory
HOPER John jun(Cuckfield)	*Solicitor. A Tory*
KING John/12(Cliffe)	Liberal
LEVETT George/12(St John)	Liberal
MORETON William/12	Liberal
MORRIS James/12	Liberal. Mr Durrant's Tenant
PENFOLD William/12	Liberal
PUMPHREY George/12	Liberal
REED Thomas/12	Liberal
ROBINSON Charles/12	Liberal
ROGERS Thos jun/3(Kingston)	Under Mr Hurley's influence
SCOBELL Rev John/13(St Ann)	A Tory
VERRALL Harry/12	Liberal
VERRALL William sen/13	A Tory
WELLER Isiah/12	Liberal
WEST Rev Harry/13(Berwick)	A Tory

LINDFIELD - 18

ALLEN Benjamin
BASHFORD John/13
BLEACK William/12
BURNETT John/12
COMBER Thomas/12
COMPTON Thomas/12
COPELAND John
COPPARD John/12(Wivelsfield)
DRAWBRIDGE William/12
HUMPHREYS Edward*/3(Brighton)
MILLS Simon/12
MORLEY Henry/12
NOYES Thomas Herbert
PIM James/12
PODMORE Henry*/12
RIDGE Thomas/12

NAME	NAME OF LANDLORD AND/OR OBSERVATIONS
TUPPEN Richard Stapely/12	
WOOD Robert/12	

LITLINGTON - 3

JENNER Thomas/1   Tenant to the Rev Thomas Scutt
SCUTT Rev Thomas   *Dead*
TERRY Charles/12(Winchelsea)

LITTLE HORSTED - 5

MARTIN John
MOON Thomas Trill
SIMPSON Rev Joseph/3
SKINNER James/12
THATCHER Thomas/13   Tenant to Lord Gage

LULLINGTON - 1

WOODHAMS Walter/13   Tenant to Earl Plymouth

MARESFIELD - 24

ATTREE Samuel/13
DAY William/3(Rotherfield)
DIVES James/13
GASSTON Edward
HILL Joseph/3
HOOKE John/13(All Saints)
JENNER Robert(Buxted)
LAURENCE John/13
MANNINGTON Richard/3
MARTEN Joseph/3
MITCHELL James/12
PAGE Edward/3
RICHARDSON Thomas/13
SIMES Tilden
TYLER Jacob*/2
TYLER John
TURNER William/13
WALTER John/13
WARNER George/13
WELLER David/13
WILDISH William/13
WINN William/13
WOOD William/13
WOODWARD Rev George

NAME	NAME OF LANDLORD AND/OR OBSERVATIONS
	MAYFIELD - 84
AVERY Thomas/12	Tenant of General Trevor's
BAKER John/12	Independent
BAKER Michael/3	Tenant of W Day Esq
BAKER Samuel/12	Independent
BASSETT John/12	Independent
BENEY Benjamin/12	Independent
BOARER John/3	Influenced by the Rev J Kirby by mis-take omitted to vote for Mr Cavendish
BRIDGER Edward/12	Independent
BRIDGER John jun/12	Independent
BRIDGER Thomas*/13	Independent
BROOK Samuel/3	Tenant
BRYANT John/12	Tenant. Independent
BRYANT John/13	Independent
BUSS Benjamin	*Independent*
BUSS John/12	Independent
CARD John/3	Influenced by W Day Esq
CARTER William/23	Independent
CHATFIELD Nicholas/23	Tenant of and influenced by Rev J Kirby
CORNWELL John Smith/12	Independent Radical
CORNWELL Robert/3(Heathfield)	Independent
DAMPER James/12	Independent
DURRANT Thomas Parker*/13	Tenant of General Trevor
FENNER James/13	Independent. Second vote influenced by Rev J Kirby
FENNER Thomas/12	Independent
FIELD Benjamin/12	Independent
FIELD William/12	Tenant of J T Weston Esq
FIELD William/12	Tenant to J Fry Esq
FOARD John/12	Independent
FOARD Thomas/12	Independent
FORTH George Eyre/12	Independent
FRY John/12	Independent
FRY John/13	Influenced in his second vote by Rev J Kirby
FRY Richard/2	Independent
FRY Robert	*Independent*
GILBERT William/12	Independent
HALL Henry/23	Influenced by J Kirby
HOLMES William/12	Tenant to W O Stone
HOSMAN George/12	Under General Trevor's Influence. Liberal
HURSELL Jonathan	*Liberal. Influenced by B Tompset*

NAME	NAME OF LANDLORD AND/OR OBSERVATIONS
JENNER John/13	Liberal. Tenant of J A Dalrymple Esq not influenced
JENNER Samuel/12	Independent
KEMP William/12	Independent
KING Zachariah/12	Independent
KIRBY Rev John/3	A Tory
KNIGHT Arthur/12	Tenant of Thomas Bridger
LADE Luke/13	Independent
LAWRENCE George*/12	Independent
MANN William/1	Tenant to J A Dalrymple Esq
MARCHANT John/12	Independent
MARCHANT Thomas/2	Independent intended to vote for Mr Cavendish
MARCHANT William/12	Independent
MILLER David/12	Liberal an old Sergeant of General Trevor's
NOAKES John*/12	Independent. Tenant of General Trevor
OLIVE John/2	Independent
PACKHAM John/3	Influenced by T P Durrant his neighbour
PACKHAM Richard/12	Independent Radical
PACKHAM Samuel/3	Independent Liberal
PAINE John/12	Tenant of S Camden will never vote for a Tory
PARRIS Thomas	
PERRSGLOVE Henry/3	Tenant of Rev J Kirby
PIPER James*/12	Independent
PIPER Joseph/12	Independent
PIPER Thomas/13	Independent. General Trevor's Tenant
PIPER William*/13	Independent
RICHARDSON Samuel/13	Influenced in second vote by Mr T P Durrant
ROCHESTER David/13	Tenant of General Trevor
ROSE Alexander/12	Independent
ROSE John/12	Tenant of A Dalrymple Esq
RUSSELL Thomas	*Tenant of W Day Esq no Tory*
RUSSELL William/3	Influenced by G W Day Esq
SHOEBRIDGE Richard/12	Independent
SMITH Henry/12	Independent
STONE Nicholas/13	Independent
STONE William Owen	*Independent. No Tory*
TOMPSETT Benjamin/3	Independent
TOMPSETT John/23	Independent
TOOTH William/12	Independent
TURK John/13	Independent

NAME	NAME OF LANDLORD AND/OR OBSERVATIONS
WALLIS Michael/12	Independent
WALTER Thomas/3	Independent
WELLER John Sawyer	*Independent*
WESTON Joel/12	Independent
WESTON Thomas/3	Tenant of Woodward Esq
WESTON William/13	Parish Clerk influenced in 2nd vote by Mr J Kirby

MOUNTFIELD - 3

HILDER Thomas/12	Independent
SMITH Tilden jun	*Independent. Tenant of Lord Ashburnham*
SMITH Tilden sen/12	Independent

NEWHAVEN - 15

BROOK Robert/12	Independent. Mr Cavendish's Canvasser
BROOKER Richard/13	Independent
COLE William/12	In employ at Customs
DOUGHTY H Hepworth/12 (Denton)	J H Bates' Tenant
EAGLES Thomas Hadlow/12	Independent
ELPHICK William/12	Independent
FAULCONER Thos Chippen*/12	Independent
KNIGHT William/12	Under Mr Elphick's influence
SMITH Rev John/13	A Tory
SMITH Henry/12	Bridge Inn under Mr Faulconer's influence
STONE Thomas/12(Brighton)	Under Mr Brooker's influence
STONE William/12	Under Mr Elphick's influence
TOWNER Charles William/12	White Hart Inn under Mr Faulconer's influence
VINALL Edward/12	Independent
WILLARD Nicholas/12	Lord Sheffield's Tenant

NEWICK - 20

ALLEN William/12	Independent
ATTREE Thomas/12	Independent. Influenced by Mr W Sturt
COLLINGS Thomas/12	Independent
DUDENEY Philip	*Lord Sheffield's Tenant*
ELLIS Isaac	*J H Slater's Tenant*
ELLIS John/12	Captain Richardson
HALL Henry jun*/12	Independent
HALL John*/12	Independent
HAMSHAR Edward/12	J H Slater's Tenant
HARMER John/12	Independent
HART Edward	*Independent*
HOLFORD Thomas/12	Independent

59

NAME	NAME OF LANDLORD AND/OR OBSERVATIONS
ISARD William/12	Independent
MORRIS Philip/12	Independent
POWELL Rev Thomas Baden/13	Independent
SHIFFNER Henry/13(Hamsey)	Under influence of the Palace
STANDEN John/12	Independent
STURT John/12	Independent
STURT William/12	Independent
THOMSON William/13	Independent

NEWTIMBER - 3

BINE Stephen(Keymer)	*Tenant of Lord Egremont*
GORDON Charles	*Owner & Independent*
TAPSELL Francis/12	Tenant of Mr Gordon

NINFIELD - 12

COLEMAN Hugh*/12	Independent
COLLINS Christopher	*Post Master also Tenant of Inn under Mr Breed's Hastings*
CRISFORD Henry/12	Independent. Tenant of Earl of Ashburnham
DAVEY George/12	Independent
FARMER John/12	Independent
HOLLAND Henry/12	Independent. Tenant to R.K. Sampson Esq
HOLLAND James/12	Independent
MORRIS Thomas/12	Independent
SAMPSON William/12	Independent
WATERS John/12	Tenant of J. Fuller Esq
WILLARD Frederick/12(All Saints,Lewes)	Independent
WRENN Walter/12	Independent. Occupies his own property & also Tenant of Col. Pilkington

NORTHIAM - 31

AUSTEN Edmund/3	Tory Landlord
BEALE James/2	Whig
BISHOPP George	*Tory Landlord*
BROWNE Edward Wright	*Tory*
COLEMAN Joseph/12	Whig
COMPORT John/12	Whig
COPPINGER Thomas/12	Whig
ELFICK William/12	Whig
ELLIOTT Henry*/12	Whig
FARRANCE Thomas/2	Whig
FIELD Thomas/12	Whig

NAME	NAME OF LANDLORD AND/OR OBSERVATIONS
GIBBS Joseph/12	Whig
GILBERT John/12	Whig
HARRIS John/2	Whig
HILDER Edward	*Tory Landlord*
LARKIN Thomas*/12	Whig
LORD Edward/13	Whig
LORD Rev Henry/13	Tory
LUXFORD Joseph/12	Whig
PARSONS William/12(Beckley)	Whig
PEENE William/12	Whig
PERIGOE William/2	doubtful
PIX John/12	Whig
RANGER George/23	Whig
ROOTS Thomas	*Tory Landlord*
SHARPE Hercules/12	Whig
SELMES James/12	Whig
SPRINGETT George/23	Tory
TRESS Francis/12	Whig
TURNER Thomas Frewin	*Tory*
WOOD Richard/12	Whig

ORE - 15

There are but 2 Votes in this Parish under any direct
Influence & the controlling power is vested in Mr. Wood of
Lewes as to one & in Mr. Shadwell as to the other. Three
individuals are Tories the rest of liberal Politics but out
of the three Tory two voted for Mr. Cavendish and are
likely to do it again. Mr. Shadwell has perhaps some
indirect influence.

BRISCO Musgrave
EASTON Joseph/12
ELIOTT William Granville*/12
ELPHINSTONE Howard/12(St Mary in the Castle, Hastings)
FEARON Rev Devey M.D./13
GORDON Cosmo/13
NASH S L (St Mary in the Castle, Hastings)
PHILIPS Henry/3
PUTLAND James/12(Beckley)
STACE John/12(St Clement, Hastings)
STACE John jun/12
WARD Thomas Newman(Udimore)
WOODROFFE William/12
WYATT Henry Early
YATES William Laurence/12

NAME	NAME OF LANDLORD AND/OR OBSERVATIONS

OVINGDEAN - 2

| KEMP Nathaniel/13 | Ind. Uncle to the Member for Lewes |
| MARSHALL Rev John/13 | Independent |

PATCHAM - 9

AYLING John/12	Tenant of Mr Rowe
BALLARD Richard*/13	Independent
BLAKER George/13	Independent
BOTTING William/13	Tenant of Mr Rowe
NEWMAN Charles/12	Tenant of Mr Rowe
PAINE John	*Independent. His mother has married Mr Hoper sen of Lewes*
SCRASE Thomas/12	Tenant of Lord Abergavenny
TANNER William	*Tenant of Lord Abergavenny*
TILLSTONE Richard Monkhouse	Independent

PEASMARSH - 24

ASHDOWN Thomas/12	Whig
BANNISTER William/12	Whig
BUTCHER William/12	Whig
CARE John/12(Iden)	Whig
CRUTTENDEN William/12	Whig
CURTEIS Herbert Barrett/1	Whig
DUNK George/12	Whig
EDMONDS William/12	Whig
GREENLAND George/12	Whig
HORTON Robert*/12(Wartling)	Whig
MORRIS William jun/12(Iden)	Tory
MORRIS William sen/12	Tory
PIX Thomas/23	Tory
PIX Thomas Smith/23(Iden)	Tory
SMITH John/12	Whig
SMITH Samuel/12	Whig
STANDEN Isaac/12	Whig
STANDEN Samuel/12	Whig
STONESTREET John/12	Whig
THOMAS Edward Smith/12	Whig
TICEHURST Moses Cleave/12	Whig
WAIT Richard/12	Whig
WIMARK John/12	Whig
WOOLLET Thomas/12	Whig

PENHURST - 3

BARROW Stephen	*Tenant of Lord Ashburnham*
SINDEN Joseph/3	Tenant of Lord Ashburnham
SMITH Tilden/12	Ind. Tenant of Lord Ashburnham

NAME	NAME OF LANDLORD AND/OR OBSERVATIONS

PETT - 6

CRUTTENDEN Thomas
OVERY Thomas
THORPE Ades Edwin
THORPE John/13
WILDISH William/12
WINCH Rev Henry/3

PEVENSEY - 8

AVERY James/12	Uninfluenced
AVERY Robert/12(Wartling)	Uninfluenced
GURR Richard/12(Pevensey	Influenced by Edward Copper of
& Westham)	Westham
HOLLAND John/12	Influenced by Mr Milward of Hastings
PHILLIPS John/12	Uninfluenced
PLUMLEY Alfred/12	Uninfluenced
PLUMLEY Thomas/12	Uninfluenced
RUSSELL John/12	Uninfluenced

PIDDINGHOE - 3

CROFT Hugh/3	Lord Chichester's Tenant
TOMSETT Joseph/12	Lord Chichester's Tenant
WATERMAN Edward/13	Independent

PIECOMBE - 4

BLAKER Nathaniel/1	Tenant of W.S. Poyntz Esq
BROWN William/12	Tenant of N. Borrer Esq
CARTER Thomas/12	
DENCH James/12	

PLAYDEN - 4

COLLYER Ralph/12	Whig
EDMONDS James/12(Rye)	Whig
ELLIOTT James/2(Iden)	Whig
PILCHER Charles/12	Whig

PLUMPTON - 1

HAINES William/12	Has left J.M. Cripps

PORTSLADE - 12

ARNOLD John/13	Independent
BLAKER Thomas/13	Independent
BORRER John*/3	Independent
FULLER Hugh/13	Independent

NAME	NAME OF LANDLORD AND/OR OBSERVATIONS
GODDARD Thomas/13	Independent
HALL John/12	Independent
HOPER Rev Henry/13	Son of Mr Hoper of Lewes
HUGGETT William/13	Independent
MOTT Luke/13	Independent
PETERS John/13	Independent
PETERS Thomas/13	Independent
WALLIS John	*Independent*

POYNINGS - 7

DODD Rev Henry Hayman (Arlington)	*Independent*
GRAIMES James/12	Independent
GUMBRELL Samuel/12	Independent
HARDWICK William/12	Independent
HOLLANDS Samuel Red	*Independent*
HOLLINGDALE William (Brighton)	*Independent*
VALLANCE J B/12	Tenant of W J Poyntz Esq

PRESTON - 4

SMITHERS Bartholomew
SMITHERS Bartholomew jun
STANFORD William
STANFORD William jun/12

RINGMER - 23

BANNISTER John/12	
BANNISTER Thomas/12	
BERRY Henry/12	
BERRY William/12	
BERRY Henry Ebenezer(Southmalling)	
CATT Edmund	
CONSTABLE Rev John/13	
EDWARDS James/12	
ELLMAN George(Glynde)	
GREENFIELD William/12	Parish Clerk
HODD Richard/12	lost his qualification
LAURENCE Thomas/13	
LUPTON Rev John	
MARTIN David/12	
MARTIN Henry/13	Earl of Plymouth's Tenant
MARTIN William jun/12	
MARTIN William sen/12	
MERRICKS James/12	

NAME	NAME OF LANDLORD AND/OR OBSERVATIONS
PAINE Henry	*Tenant of Sir James Langham*
RICKMAN John*/12	
STANFORD Charles/12	
VERRALL G.H./12(Ringmer & Cliffe)	
WELLER Henry/12	

RIPE - 9

CANE Edward/12
CANE William/12
FEIST William/12
GEALL John/12
MANNINGTON Matthew/12
MARTIN William/12
RAYNES Rev William/13
WEEDEN Thomas/12
WELLER James/12

RODMELL - 5

FEARS William/13	Under influence of H. Hurley & J. Saxby
MARTEN John/12	Independent
PLUMER Charles/3(Southease)	Lord Abergavenny's Tenant
SAXBY Charles/13	Lord Abergavenny's Tenant
SAXBY John/13	Lord Abergavenny's Tenant

ROTHERFIELD - 55

Those votes marked thus X and perhaps a few others in Rotherfield Parish being Tenants or dependents of Lord Abergavenny would probably vote as he wished.

Messrs. Stone canvassed Rotherfield over & over again very carefully & there seemed to prevail a very strong feeling of Independence & in favour of Reform of all kinds.

Two or three voters were tried very hard by Tory influence and refrained from voting altogether rather than vote against the Reform Candidates.

A more influential Tory might perhaps obtain 6 Votes but not more unless he had the Influence of Lord Abergavenny.

ALLCORN William
BABINGTON Thomas
BARNES Thomas/12
BRYANT William/12
BRYANT William/12

NAME	NAME OF LANDLORD AND/OR OBSERVATIONS
CAMFIELD George X/12	
COCHRAN John/12	
COLE William X/12	
CORKE Benjamin/12	
CRAWLEY Rev Richard	
CRITTALL Robert/12	
DADSWELL Alfred Taylor X/12	
DADSWELL David Taylor X/12	
DADSWELL Robert X/12	
FIELD Thomas	
FIELD William/12	
HIDER William	
IZZARD James/12	
JARVIS William*/2	
KENWARD Henry/12	
KILLICK John/12	
LANGRIDGE John	
LEONARD Thomas/12	
LOCKYER John/12	
LOCKYER Thomas/12	
LULHAM Benjamin/12	
MAPLESDEN William/12	
MILES Michael/12	
MOON William/12	
NEWNHAM John	
PAIGE Edward/12	
PAINE Henry/12	
PEERLESS William/12	
ROGERS William/12	
SALES Samuel/12	
SALTER James/12	
STAPLEY John Baker/12	
THWAITES Henry	
TURNER Rev John Jarvis	
VINALL John/12	A Whig
WALTER Edward/12(Wadhurst)	
WALTER William/12	
WICKENDEN William/12	
WICKENDEN William	
WICKENS Benjamin/12	
WICKENS George	
WICKENS James/12	
WICKENS John/12	
WICKENS Joseph/12	
WICKENS Joseph	

NAME	NAME OF LANDLORD AND/OR OBSERVATIONS
WICKENS Joseph/12	
WICKENS Samuel/12	
WICKENS Thomas/12	
WICKENS Thomas	
WILSON John/12	

ROTTINGDEAN - 10

BEARD Charles/12	Tenant of Lord Abergavenny but Independent
BEARD Stenning/12	Independent. Tenant of Lord Abergavenny
BEARD Thomas/12	Independent
D'OYLY Thomas*/1	Independent
DUMBRELL William/12	Independent
FARNCOMBE John*/12	Tenant of Lord Abergavenny
HOOKER Rev T Redman D.D./2	Independent
HUTCHINGS Rev James/3 (Telscombe)	Independent. A Tory
INGRAM James/13	Independent
RICHARDSON Thomas/12	Independent

RYE - 72

ALCE Robert/13	Whig
ALLEN Justinian/13	Whig
AMON John	*Whig*
AMOS Thomas/13	Whig
AYLWARD Charles	*Whig*
AYLWARD Thomas William/12	Whig
AYLWARD William/12	Whig
BACK Usher/12	Whig
BARRY Frederick/12	Whig
CHAMBERLAYNE Stanes Brocket	*Whig*
CHATTERTON Edward	*Tory*
CHATTERTON William(Win-chelsea)	*Whig*
CLARK John/12	Whig
CLARK Thomas/13	Whig
CLARK Thomas	*Whig*
COLLINS George/13	Whig
CROSSKEY William	*Whig*
CURD William*/12	Whig
DAWES Edward Nathaniel*/2 (Playden)	Tory
DAWES Weeden/2(Playden)	Tory
ELLENDEN James*/12	Whig

NAME	NAME OF LANDLORD AND/OR OBSERVATIONS
FIELD James/13	Whig
FRENCH Charles/12	Whig
FRISE George/13	Whig
FRYMAN Charles Kennett/12	Whig
GIBBON Thomas/13	Whig
GILES John/13	Whig
GILL Daniel/12	Dead
HATTER Thomas/12	Whig
HATTER William/12	Whig
HAYWARD Thomas/13	Whig
HEATH Richard/12	Whig
HESSELL James/12	Whig
HICKS Charles/12	Whig
HILDER Edward*/12	Whig
HOLLIS William/12	Whig
HOLLOWAY William/12	Whig
HONEYSETT David/13(Guestling)Whig	
HUGGINS William Oliver/13	Whig
HUNTER William	*Whig*
JARRETT William/12	Whig
JUBB William/13	Whig
LARDNER John Haddock	*Whig*
LAWRENCE Charles/1	Whig
LEAVER Thomas/12	Whig
MANSER David sen/13	Whig
MARLEY George William/12	Whig
MERYON John*/12	Whig
MILLS Joseph/12	Whig
PIPER Jesse/12(Salehurst)	Whig
POMFRET Richard Curteis/2 (Iden)	Tory
PROCTOR Thomas/13	Tory
RAMSDEN William/12	Whig
SELMES James/12(Northiam)	Whig
SEYMOUR James/12	Whig
SHARWELL William/13	Whig
SKINNER George	*Whig*
SMITH Jeremiah/12(Rye, Udimore & Eastbourne)	Whig
SMITH William*/1	Whig
TAYLOR David*/2	Whig
THOMAS Charles/12	Whig
THOMAS Charles jun/12	Whig
THORPE Thomas/12	Whig
TURNER Francis/13	Whig

NAME	NAME OF LANDLORD AND/OR OBSERVATIONS
VENNELL Thomas/13(Playden)	Whig
VIDLER John*/12	Whig
WATERS Edward/12	Whig
WOOD Thomas/12	Whig
WOOD William/12	Whig
WOOLLETT William/13	Whig
WORSELL Richard/12	Whig
WRIGHT James/13	Whig

SALEHURST - 48

Mr James Hilder the Banker & Mr Tilden Smith of Mountfield also Banker have great influence in this Parish.

ADAMS Henry/2	Labourer, works for J Hilder Influenced by Mr Hilder
ADAMS Thomas/3	Clerk. Influenced by Mr Hilder
BROCKHURST Richard/13	Labourer, works for Mr Alfrey Influenced by Mr Alfrey
BUSS John/12	Butcher. Independent
BUSS Thomas/12	Farmer. S.B. Micklethwaite Esq, would not wish to oppose Landlord
CAMPANY John/12	Farmer. Wilson Esq. Influenced by Mr Wilson
CROFT Edward/12	Yeoman. Influenced by Mr Luxford
CRUTTENDEN John/12	Farmer. His Brother. Independent
DAVENPORT Richard/12	Esquire. Himself. Independent
DETRAZAYLLE Peter Ct.	*Gentleman. Himself. Independent*
ELPHEE Henry/12(Etchingham)	Farmer. Independent
ERRY Joseph/3(Warbleton)	[Farmer & Carpenter Influenced by Mr Micklethwait]
GARNER George jun/12 (Etchingham)	Farmer. S.B. Micklethwaite Esq. Influenced by him
HARTNUP Thomas	*Farmer. S.B. Micklethwaite Esq. Independent*
HEATHFIELD Edward/12	Yeoman. Independent
HILDER James/12	Banker. Independent
HILDER John/12	Gentleman. Independent
HOW Samuel/3	Innkeeper. Independent
JONES Robert/2	Auctioneer. Influenced by Mr Hilder
LUSTED Thomas/23	Shoemaker. Independent
LUXFORD John/12	Esquire. Independent
MARCHANT Robert/12	Tailor. Independent
MARTIN Henry/12	Blacksmith. Influenced by Mr Hilder
MARTIN Thomas/12	Farmer. Mr Micklethwaite. Not influenced

69

NAME	NAME OF LANDLORD AND/OR OBSERVATIONS
MERRITT Edward/12	Carpenter. Influenced by his Customers
MICKLETHWAIT Sotherton B P	Esquire. Independent
MILLS John/12	Shopkeeper. Independent
MUNN Thomas*/12	Salesman. Independent
NASH John/12	Nurseryman. Independent
NICHOLLS James/12	Labourer works for Mr Hilder Influenced by Mr Hilder
NOAKES Joseph Elias*/12 (Lamberhurst	Innkeeper. Influenced by Mr Hilder
PEMBLE Paul/12	Breechesmaker. Independent
PIPER John/12	Bricklayer would go with the majority
PUTLAND Henry	Shopkeeper. Independent
RUSSELL Samuel	Shoemaker. Independent
SIMMONS John/12	Farmer. Mr J Hilder. Has left
SMITH Benjamin/12	Gentleman. Independent
SMITH James/12	Spirit Merchant. Influenced by Mr Hilder
SMITH Stephen/12(Bodiam)	Farmer. Influenced by J Smith his father
STANDEN Henry/3	Bricklayer. Influenced by Mr Darby
TINDELL Stephen/12	Farmer. Influenced by Mr Hilder
WATERS Joseph/12	Nurseryman. Influenced by Mr Hilder
WEEKS Thomas	Postmaster. Influenced by Mr Hilder
WELLER William/12	Farmer. Independent
WESTON Henry/12	Butcher would go with the stream
WRENCH Rev Jacob George/3	Vicar. Independent. a Tory
YOUNG William*/12	Clerk to Mr J Hilder. Influenced by Mr Hilder

SEAFORD - 23

ALLWORK Thomas/12	Uninfluenced
ALLWORK Thomas jun*/12	Uninfluenced
BEAL Richard/1	Uninfluenced
BROOKER James/12	Uninfluenced
BULL Henry/13	Uninfluenced
BULL Thomas Henry/13	Uninfluenced
CARNEGIE Rev James/13	Uninfluenced
CHAMBERS Thomas William/12	Tenant of Lord Chichester
CHAMPION William/13	Uninfluenced
COLWELL James/13	Uninfluenced
EVANS John*/12(Hurst- pierpoint)	Uninfluenced
EVES Stephen/13	Uninfluenced
GODDEN Edward/13(Hailsham)	Uninfluenced
GORRING James/13	Uninfluenced
GORRING Thomas/13	Uninfluenced

NAME	NAME OF LANDLORD AND/OR OBSERVATIONS
KING John/13	Tenant of Charles Harrison Esq
LIDBETTER Thomas	*Uninfluenced*
REDMAN Richard/13	Influenced by King & Lidbetter
ROBERTS Daniel	*Uninfluenced*
SIMMONS James/12	Uninfluenced
STEVENS Joseph/12	Uninfluenced
TOWNER William/13	Uninfluenced
VERRAL Charles/12	Uninfluenced

SEDDLESCOMB - 15

BISHOP John	*Independent*
BUTLER Philip/12	Independent
BYNER Thomas/12	Independent
COSSUM Richard*/12 (Hollington)	Independent
CRISFORD Spencer/12	Independent
DENNETT Thomas/12	Independent
ELDRIDGE William jun	*Independent*
ELDRIDGE William sen	*Independent works for Mr Briscoe Esq*
GRACE Henry/12	Independent
GRACE William/12	Independent
MERCER Richard	*Independent*
PRATT Rev John/13	Independent
SIMES John	*Tenant of late Duchess of Dorset's Farm*
WESTON James*/12	Independent
WESTON Robert/12	Independent

SELMESTON - 1

FULLER Joseph(Waldron)

SLAUGHAM - 8

BLAKE Robert Dudley	*unknown generally resides in London*
ELLYATT John/12	Independent
HASLEWOOD William/12	
HEAVER William/2	under the sole influence of Mr Sergison his Landlord
JENNER William/12	Independent
LEWRY William/2	under the sole influence of Mr Sergison his Landlord
SUGDEN Sir Edward Burtenshaw knt	
YOUNG Thomas/12	Independent

SOUTHEASE - 3

FUNNELL William Baker/12	Independent influenced by W Verrall
KENT James/3	Under influence of Hurly Ingram Harman
KENT John/3	Under influence of Hurly Ingram Harman

NAME	NAME OF LANDLORD AND/OR OBSERVATIONS

STANMER - 1

WOODMAN Richard/1   Lord Chichester's Tenant

STREET - 3

FITZHUGH Rev William   *Liberal*
    Anthony
STURT William/13   Tenant of J H Lane
TROWER John/13   Under H Hurly's influence

TARRING NEVILLE - 2

FULLER Robert/12
RANGER George/12   Influenced by Mr Fuller

TELSCOMBE - 3

KENT George/3   Under Mr J Kent & H Roger's influence
OSBORNE William*/12   Tenant of Lord Delawarr
TOMPSETT James/12   under influence of his father

TICEHURST - 60

ADAMS John/12   Gentleman. Independent
AUSTIN James   *Farmer. Rev R Wetherall. Influenced by him but would not vote*
BAKER John/12   Farmer. Himself. Independent
BALCOMB Richard/3   Bricklayer works for Mr Wetherell. Influenced by him
BARDEN Thomas/12   Farmer. Mr S Baker would go as his Landlord wishd
BARROW Richard/12   Farmer. Rev T Coney. Independent
BLACKMAN Samuel   *Servant to Sir G Thomas. Influenced by his Master*
BOORMAN Samuel   *Farmer. Richard Preston Esq. Independent*
BRISSENDEN William/12   Farmer. Independent
BUCKLAND John/12   Farmer. Thomas Glanville Esq. Ind
BUSS Benjamin/12   Farmer. Himself. Independent
CHILD Joseph/3   Carpenter. Influenced by Mr Wetherell
CLAPSON Francis/3   Tailor. Influenced by Mr Wetherell
COURTHOPE George/13   Esquire. Himself. Independent
DITCH John/2   Farmer. Mr Wetherell. Independent
ELLIOTT William/3   Shoemaker. Influenced by Mr Wetherell
FARRANCE John/12   Farmer. J Roberts Esq. Independent
FRENCH James/12   Shoemaker. Independent
GLANVILLE Thomas William   *Esquire. Independent*
HARRIS William/12   Common Carrier. Independent

NAME	NAME OF LANDLORD AND/OR OBSERVATIONS
HODGE George/3	Bricklayer. Influenced by Mr C Newington
HUNTLEY Thomas/23	Miller. Influenced by Mr C Newington
HYLAND William/12	Schoolmaster
JARVIS Gideon/12	Farmer. Independent
JARVIS Thomas	*Farmer. Rev R Wetherell. Influenced by his Landlord not to vote for Mr Cavendish & Curteis*
JUDGE Thomas	*Parish Clerk. Influenced by his Landlord not to vote for Mr Cavendish & Curteis*
KEMP George/3	Glazier. Influenced by his Landlord & Mr C Newington
KEMP Henry/3	Carpenter. Mr C Newington
MARCHANT Jesse/12	Farmer. Forbes Esq. Indepedent
NEWINGTON Charles/3	Surgeon. Himself. Independent a Tory
NEWINGTON George/3	Farmer
NEWINGTON Joel/12	Miller. Independent
NEWINGTON Thomas/12	Farmer. Mr A Playsted. Independent
NOAKES Henry/12	Farmer. Himself. Independent
NOAKES William/12	Draper & Grocer. Himself. Independent
OYLER George	*Farmer. Mr Constable. Influenced by Mr Wetherell not to vote for Cavendish & Curteis*
PULLINGER John/3	Wheelwright. Influenced by Mr Wetherell not to vote for Cavendish & Curteis
READ Peter/3	Farmer. G Courthope Esq. Influenced by Mr Courthope not to vote for Cavendish & Curteis
ROGERS James/12	Farmer. James Rogers. Independent
SIGGS Samuel/3	Labourer. works for Mr C Newington. Influenced by him
SIVYER John jun/12	Assistant overseer. Independent
SIVYER John sen/12	Innkeeper. Himself. Independent
SMITH Robert/12	Farmer. Independent
STANBRIDGE Benjamin	*Farmer. J Roberts Esq. Influenced by Mr Roberts not to vote for Cavendish & Curteis*
STANDEN John/12	Farmer. Himself. Independent
STANDEN John	*Butcher. Influenced by Mr Wetherell*
STANDEN Stephen/3	Farmer. Mr Wetherell. Influenced by Mr Wetherell
STANDEN Thomas	*Butcher. Influenced by Mr Wetherell not to vote for Cavendish & Curteis*

NAME	NAME OF LANDLORD AND/OR OBSERVATIONS
STEVINSON Stephen/12	Farmer. Independent
TAPSELL Richard/12	Draper & Grocer. Independent
TOMSETT James/12	Farmer. Himself. Independent
VIDLER William/12	Farmer. R K Sampson Esq. Independent
WAGHORN George/3	Carpenter. Influenced by Mr Wetherell
WAGHORN Thomas/3	Carpenter. Influenced by Mr Wetherell
WAGHORN Thomas/12	Farmer. G Courthope Esq. Influenced by Mr Wetherell his Landlord
WALKER Joseph/1	Innkeeper. J Roberts Esq. Independent
WATSON Daniel/12	Farmer. Independent
WETHERELL Rev Richard/3	Vicar a Tory & Brother to Sir Charles Wetherell
WHITE Stephen	*Farmer. G Courthope Esq. Influenced by him not to vote against Darby*
WINCH John/12	Farmer. Independent

TWINEHAM - 6

BOTTING John/12
BROAD James/13
DAVEY Edmund
GORING Rev Charles
SHARP William/12
WALDER Samuel/13

UCKFIELD - 38

BERWICK Thomas/12(Buxted)
BEST James/12
CAMERON James/12(Maresfield)
CHEALE Alexander/12(Southover)
COVEY William Henry/3
EADES George
FENNER William*/12
FOSTER John Henry/12(Framfield)
FOWLE William/12(Brighton)
GOSLING William/12
GOSLING William/12(Waldron)
HARMER John/12
HARTLEY John
HASTINGS Thomas Martin/12   Influenced by Mr Mabbott
HOW William/12   Influenced by Mr Mabbott
HURDIS George Clarke
JENNER John/12
KENWARD Edward/12
KENWARD John/12

KENWARD William/12
LIDBETTER George/12
LIDBETTER Samuel/12
LIDBETTER William Henry*/12
MABBOTT William Courthope*/12
MANNINGTON George
MANNINGTON John jun
MARKWICK John/12
MERRICKS Thomas jun/12
NEWNHAM John/12
PERIGOE Samuel/12(Hailsham)
PRINCE Charles/12
ROGERS Edward/12(Buxted)
SHEPHARD Thomas/12
SMITH William/3
STREATFIELD Richard Shuttleworth/12
UNDERWOOD Rev John/3
WATERMAN James/12
WOODWARD John/3

UDIMORE - 5

FILMER William/12	Whig
LANGFORD Thomas Cooper*/12	Whig
(Brede)	
REEVE Lawrence(Peasmarsh)	*Tenant to a Tory Landlord*
SLOMAN John	*Whig*
WOODHAMS John/12	Whig. Tenant to a Tory Landlord

WADHURST - 50

APPS James/12	Independent
ASHBY William/13	Independent
AUSTEN Henry/12	Independent
AUSTEN Jeffery	*Tenant of Marquis Camden. no Tory*
AUSTEN Thomas	*Tenant of Marquis Camden. no Tory*
AVARD Edward	*Independent*
BALDWIN Samuel/3	Tenant of G Courthope Esq
BARTON Thomas/12	Independent
BASSETT Thomas/12	Independent
BENGE William Henry/12	Independent
BRISSENDEN Thomas/3	Tenant of G Courthope Esq
BULL Thomas	*Vestry Clerk*
CHRISMAS Joseph/12	Independent
DADSWELL Edward/3	Independent
DAVID Jonathan/12	Independent
DOWN George/12	Independent. no Tory

NAME	NAME OF LANDLORD AND/OR OBSERVATIONS
FIELD Joseph/12	Independent
FISHER William	*Independent. Postmaster*
FOWLE John/12	Independent
FRENCH William/12	Tenant of J Newington Esq
GARDINER Rev Robert Barlow	*Vicar*
GIBBS James/12	Independent
HALEY Aylmer	*Independent. Liberal*
HAMMOND Thomas/12	Independent
HARMER James/12	Tenant of G Courthope Esq
HILDER John	*Tenant of M Camden. no Tory*
HOLMAN George/12	Independent. Tenant of Rev E R Raynes
HOLMAN Jasper/2	Tenant of J Newington Esq
KINE Joseph/12	Independent
KNIGHT Thomas/3	Tenant of G Courthope Esq
LATTER Laurence	*Tenant of Mar. Camden*
MOREN William/3	Tenant of Mar. Camden
NEWINGTON John	*Independent*
PACKHAM William	*Tenant of Mar. Camden*
PIERSON Thomas/12	Tenant of Mar. Camden
PLAYSTED Alfred sen/12	Independent
PLAYSTED George Luck/12	Independent
PLAYSTED Henry jun/3	Independent
ROGERS Henry/12	Independent
ROGERS James/12	Independent
SMITH George/3	Tenant of Mar. Camden
SMITH Richard/3	
SPRINGETT John/12	Independent
STUNT Joseph/12	Independent
TOMPSETT William/12	Independent
VIGOR Richard/13	Independent
WACE Thomas	*a Tory*
WAGHORN John/23	Independent intended to vote for Cav & Darby
WALLIS John/3	Influenced by G Courthope Esq
WALLIS Samuel/3	Influenced by Mar. Camden

WALDRON - 22

AVERY Thomas/12
BONNICK Josias/12
COLMAN James/3
GILBERT William/12
GOLDSMITH Benjamin/12
HEATHFIELD John/12   works for Sir C R Blunt
JENNER James/12
JENNER Thomas/12

NAME	NAME OF LANDLORD AND/OR OBSERVATIONS
KENNARD John/12	
MANNINGTON Isaac/12	
MOON Neri/3	Influenced by the Rev T Raynes
RAYNES Rev Thomas	
REEVES John/12	
RUSSELL John/12	
RUSSELL William/12	
SANDERS John/1	
SNASHALL John/12	
THOMAS William/12	
THOMPSON William/12(Heathfield)	
WATERS Benjamin/12	
WATERS John/12	
WOOD James/12	

WARBLETON - 34

AVARD William George/3	Independent but voted for Mr Darby because he was a Neighbour
BAITUP Richard/3	Miller. Mr Henry Blackman. Influenced by Mr Darby
BALCOMB Thomas/3	Shopkeeper. Influenced by Mr Darby
BENNETT Henry/3	Shopkeeper. Influenced by Mr Darby
BLACKMAN Henry/3	Farmer. Influenced by Mr Darby
BOOTH John/3	Farmer. Influenced by Mr Darby
BURGESS James/3	Butcher. Influenced by Mr Darby
BURGESS Jeremiah/3	Innkeeper. Influenced by Mr Darby
CHAPMAN John/3	Farmer. Influenced by Mr Darby
COLE Rev Benjamin Thomas Halcot	*Rector. Influenced by Mr Darby*
CROWHURST James/3	Farrier. [J Day Esq] Influenced by Mr Darby
CRUTTENDEN Edmund/3	Farmer. J Darby Esq. Influenced by his Landlord
DALLAWAY Stephen/3	Farmer. J Day Esq. Influenced by his Landlord
DARBY George Esquire	*Candidate*
DARBY John Esquire/3	Candidate's Father
ERREY Joseph/3	Bailiff to Mr Darby. Dependent on Mr Darby
FENNER Josiah/3	Farmer. Influenced by Mr Darby
GOLDSMITH James/3	Brickmaker. Influenced by Mr Darby
HUNT Samuel/1	Shoemaker. Independent
ISTED William/12	Farmer. The Walters family E/Bourne. Influenced by Mr Darby

NAME	NAME OF LANDLORD AND/OR OBSERVATIONS
KEELEY Richard/3	Farmer. John Darby Esq. Influenced by Mr Darby
LADE Thomas/3	Farmer. John Darby Esq. Influenced by Mr Darby
LADE Vincet/3	Farmer. John Darby Esq. Influenced by Mr Darby
MARTIN Stephen/3	Farmer. J Fuller Esq. Influenced by Mr Darby
MESSAGE Thomas/3	Higler. Influenced by Mr Darby
OLLIVER Jesse/3	Farmer
PATTENDEN John	*Farmer. was induced not to vote for Cav & Cur by Ld Ashburnham's Steward*
PATTENDEN Robert/3	Farmer. John Darby Esq. Influenced by Landlord
POTTER Henry/3	Farmer. Lord Ashburnham. Influenced by Landlord
POTTER Thomas/3	Governor of Workhouse. Parish
STAR Thomas/12	Farmer. Independent
WENHAM James/3	Innkeeper & Servant to Major Fuller. Influenced by Master
WHITEMAN John/3	Farmer. Influenced by Mr Darby
WILMSHURST Stephen/3	Farmer. Influenced by Mr Darby

WARTLING - 34

AKEHURST John	*Gillon Esq*
ATWOOD Thomas/12	
BARDEN James/12	
BARNES William/12	E B Curteis Esq
BELLINGHAM James/12(Playden)	
BLACKMAN William	*E J Curteis Esq*
BRAY George*/12	Earl Ashburnham
COLLINS John/12	Earl Ashburnham
CURTEIS Edward Barratt/12(Beckley)	
CURTEIS Edward Jeremiah/12	
CURTEIS Reginald/12(Beckley)	
DAWES Alfred/2	
DAWES Joseph/12	
EDMONDS Charles/12	
ELWOOD Charles William/12	
FULLER Rev Thomas	
HALL Henry/12	
HARMER James/3	Mrs Wagner
HART Edward/12(Warbleton)	
HICKS Richard	*Earl Ashburnham*
HOLLAND Francis/12	

NAME	NAME OF LANDLORD AND/OR OBSERVATIONS
JENNER John/12	E J Curteis Esq
LADE Daniel/1	E J Curteis Esq Bramstone
LOCK William/12(Herstmonceux)	
MARCHANT Stephen/12(Herstmonceux)	
MILLER John/12	
NOAKES Henry/12	
OXLEY David	
OXLEY Nicholas	*Earl Ashburnham*
PARRIS Edward/12	Earl Ashburnham
(Herstmonceux)	
PINYON Thomas/12	
THORPE Thomas/12	E J Curteis
WENHAM James	
WOODHAMS John/12	E J Curteis Esq

WEST DEAN - 5

ADE Charles/12	Tenant of Rev W Scutt of Clapham
ELLIS John/3	Tenant of Lord Gage
ELLIS John jun	*Tenant of Lord Gage*
NEWMAN William/12	Tenant of Rev W Scutt
SAXBY Richard*/12	Tenant of Earl Burlington

WESTFIELD - 24

The chief Landowners are Dr Lamb (Rye) Mr Briscoe
(Hastings) Mr Benjamin Smith (Salehurst) & Miss Milward
several small owners are voters - The Parish on the
aggregate is likely to continue friendly to the Whig
Interest.

BAKER Robert
BAKER Thomas/12
BAKER William
BAKER William jun
BRAY George/12
BROOK John/12
CATT John/2
CATT Stephen/12
CATT William/3
CRISFORD Stephen/12
CRISFORD Stephen jun/12
CRUTTENDEN Tilden (Rejected)
GILL Gideon/12
HYLAND John/12
MAWLE John/12
MERCER Joseph/12
NOAKES Robert/12

NAME	NAME OF LANDLORD AND/OR OBSERVATIONS
OSBORNE David/12	
SELMES James/12	
SELMES Stephen/12	
STUNT Thomas jun/12	
STUNT Thomas sen/12	
TYHURST John/12	
WELLER John/12	

WEST FIRLE - 7

BERRY George/13	Tenant to Lord Gage
ELLIS Charles M/3	Tenant to Lord Gage
HILLMAN John/13	Tenant to Lord Gage
HUTCHENSON Rev Charles Edward/13	
LANGRIDGE John/1	
SAXBY William*/3	
STEPHENS John/1	Tenant to Lord Gage

WESTHAM - 29

ARKCOLL William/12	Tenant of Earl of Liverpool
BRETON Robert/12	Tenant of Mitford Esq
COPPER Edward/12(Pevensey)	Uninfluenced
CRISFORD Samuel	*Uninfluenced*
DELVES Thomas/12	Uninfluenced
FILDER John Turner/12	Tenant of Earl of B
GRACE Rev Henry Thomas/1	Presented by Earl of B
GEERING Aaron/12	Influenced by the farmers
GEERING James/12	Influenced by the farmers
GEERING Moses/12	Influenced by the farmers
GEERING William/12	Uninfluenced
GORRINGE John/1(Hellingly)	Tenant of Earl of B
HAWES Robert/12	Tenant of Sir William Fagg
HUNT Thomas/1	Uninfluenced
KENWARD William/12	Uninfluenced
LANGFORD Charles/1	Tenant of Earl of B
LANGFORD Stephen/12	Tenent of Earl of B
LEIGH Henry/12	Uninfluenced
LEWIS Thomas/12	Influenced by Mr James Whiteman
MILLER William/12	Uninfluenced
PITCHER John/12(Hailsham)	Tenant of Earl of Liverpool
ROODS Samuel/12	Tenant of Earl of B
SPICE Henry/12	Influenced by Mr William Arckoll
SLYE Matthias*/1(Hailsham)	Uninfluenced
STREETER Nathaniel/12	Uninfluenced
WARD Henry/12	Uninfluenced
WEBB William/12	Uninfluenced

NAME	NAME OF LANDLORD AND/OR OBSERVATIONS
WHITEMAN John/1	Uninfluenced. Father of Mr Cavendish's Agent
WOODHAMS Francis/1	Uninfluenced

WESTHOATHLY - 9

CLIFFORD Thomas/12	Owner
COMBER John/12	Not influenced by his Landlord
POILE John/12	Owner
POLLARD Philip/12	Owner
STANBRIDGE Thos/12(Ardingly)Owner	
TURNER John/12	Not influenced by his Landlord
TURNER Richard/12	Not influenced by his Landlord
TURNER William/1	
WOODMAN William/12(Worth)	Owner

WESTMESTON - 5

BOTTING William/12	Independent. Tenant of J M Cripps
COURTHORPE Rev William*/3	A Tory
HODSON John	*lost his qualification. Tenant of J H Bridger*
LANE Henry Thomas/13	A Tory
SPRINGATE John/13	Tenant of J H Lane

WHATLINGTON - 7

ADES Moses/12(Sedlescomb)	Independent
BATES William/2	Independent
DAWS William/13	Independent & Tenant of Thomas Dawes of Ewhurst
DOWLING Richard/12	Independent & Owner & Landlord of Royal Oak Inn
OVERY Stephen/12	Independent
SIMS John/3	Independent & also Tenant of Lord Ashburnham
STEVENSON Thomas/3(Mayfield)	

WILLINGDON - 19

ADAMS William/12	Influenced by principal Inhabitants of Willingdon
BARTHOLOMEW William/1	Uninfluenced
CARTER Edward/1	Parish Clerk under influence of Rev Henry Moore
DENMAN Arnold*/1	Tenant of Inigo Thomas Esq
ELPHICK Henry/12	Uninfluenced
MOORE Rev Henry/1	Influenced by I Thomas Esq
NEWMAN Robert/1	Uninfluenced

NAME	NAME OF LANDLORD AND/OR OBSERVATIONS
PAGE Richard/12	Influenced by the Inhabitants particularly Mr Putland
PUTLAND John/12	Tenant of I Thomas Esq
RIPPINGTON Edward/12	Influenced by principal Inhabitants
SEYMOUR Joseph/1	Tenant of I Thomas Esq
TERRY Thomas*/12	Influenced by principal Inhabitants particularly Mr Putland
THOMAS Inigo/1	Uninfluenced
TICEHURST William/1	Influenced by I Thomas Esq
VERRELL Charles/1	Influenced by the Inhabitants particularly Mr Putland
VERRELL Henry/1	Influenced by the Inhabitants particularly Mr Putland
VINE James/1	Influenced by the Inhabitants particularly Mr Putland
WILLARD James Dippery sen/12	Uninfluenced
WILLARD James Dippery jun/12	Uninfluenced

WILMINGTON - 8

ADE James/1	
CAPPER Rev James*/1	
CROWHURST James/13	
HARMAN Samuel/12	
LAMBE John/1	Tenant to Earl of Burlington
LAMBE Richard/1	Tenant to Earl of Burlington
LAMBE William/12	Tenant to Earl of Burlington
PEERLESS William/12	Influenced by Mr Lamb

WINCHELSEA - 14

ALCE Robert/13	Whig
AUSTEN Edmund/12(Rye)	Whig
BARHAM Henry/12	Whig
FULLER Walter	Whig
HARROD George/2	Whig
HEARNDEN Isaac	Whig
HOLT Jacob/12	Whig
JONES Joash	Whig
LONGLEY William/12	Whig
NOON William/12(St Mary in the Castle)	Whig
NORLEY William/13(Rye)	Whig
OSBORNE Richard	Whig
SARGENT William/1	Whig
WEST Rev John James/12	Tory

NAME	NAME OF LANDLORD AND/OR OBSERVATIONS

WITHYHAM - 16

BALE Rev Sackville Stephens/13
BRETT John
CHAPPELL Frederick Coley
CHEWTER William/13
CORK Thomas/12
CROWHURST William/3   Earl Delawarr
CROWHURST William*/12   Independent
GILHAM William   *Independent*
HALL Obadiah/13   Earl Delawarr
MARTIN Francis/13   Earl Delawarr
PATCHING Thomas/12
PECKHAM Edmund(Rotherfield)
RICHARDSON Joseph(Buxted)
SHOESMITH Edward Sears/13
TASKER Philip
TURNER John/13   Earl Delawarr

WIVELSFIELD - 7

BACCUS William Henry*/12
COMBER Thomas/12
FARNCOMBE Joseph/12
HOMEWOOD William/12
KNIGHT Frederick/12
TANNER Richard/3
WELLS Henry/12

WORTH - 33

AKEHURST Samuel   *Promised to vote for Mr Cavendish*
BETHUNE Rev George   Agrees with Mr Cavendish in his
     Maximilian/1   Political opinions
BLUNT Francis Scawen*/13   Tory but is well known to Mr Cavendish
BRAZIER Samuel/13   Uninfluenced
BRISTOW Henry/13   Tenant to Mr Gilbert Jolliffe a Tory
CAFFIN Peter/13   Independent
CHANDLER Richard/12   Owner
CREASY Edward/12   Owner
CURZON Thomas Roper
DAVIS James/13   Independent
FULLER John/12   Independent
GRAYHAM Edward   *Independent*
HAINS Henry   *Independent*
HAINS Philip John/12   Independent
HOOKER John/12   Independent
HOOKER Thomas/12   Independent

NAME	NAME OF LANDLORD AND/OR OBSERVATIONS
HUMPHREY Thomas/12	Influenced by Dr Bethune
ILLMAN Richard/12	Independent
JEAL William/13	Independnet
JOHNSON John/12	Tenant of Gilbert Jolliffe but not influenced by Landlord
JOLIFFE Gilbert East*/3	a Tory
LUNDIE John Stow*/12	Independent
NICKALLS George/12	Independent
OUVRY John	*Declined promising Mr Cavendish*
SHEPHERD John/12	Independent
STANBRIDGE John/12	Influenced by Sir Timothy Shelley his Landlord
STARLEY Walter/12	Independent
SQUIRE William/12	Independent
TESTER James/12	Independent
TESTER William/12	Independent
VIGAR Robert/12	Independent
WALKER Peter*/12	Independent
YOUNG Henry/12	Independent

WEST SUSSEX - 55

NAME	WHERE RESIDENT	WHERE REGISTERED	OBSERVATIONS
AGATE James	*Horsham*	*Brighton*	*Reformer but unable to leave home*
BAKER John/12	Horsham	Bolney	Reformer but unable to leave home
BROOKER Henry/12	New Shoreham	Brighton	
BROWN Edward/13	Steyning	Brighton	Independent
BROWN John/12	Horsham	Ditcheling	Independent
BURRELL Sir C M bart	*Shipley*	*Southmalling*	
BURRIDGE William/12	Horsham	Brighton	Reformer
CAFFIN John/12	Ifield	Crawley	Reformer
CAMERON John Savage/12	Cowdry	Uckfield	
CAVE Michael/12	New Shoreham	Wadhurst	
CHASEMAR Philip/12	Horsham	Barcombe	Reformer
COMMERELL Jno William	*Strood*	*Worth*	*Promised to support Mr Cavendish but was disinclined to undertake the Journey*

84

NAME	WHERE RESIDENT	WHERE REGISTERED	OBSERVATIONS
CONSTABLE Rev Richard /13	Cowfold	Hailsham	Voted for Mr Darby in preference to Mr Curteis on Account of the inconsistent conduct of Mr Curteis in signing 2 company Petitions relating to the Malt Tax
COOPER Rev W Henry	Washington	Brighton	
DENNETT John	Woodmancote	Lindfield	
DICKENS Charles Scrase sen	Chichester	Brighton	
DINNAGE Joshua	Southwick	Brighton	
GELL Francis*/12	Aplesham	St Ann	
GILLAUME Thomas/13	New Shoreham	Brighton	
GORRINGE W Pennington	Southwick	Heathfield	
GORRINGE William/12	Kingston by Sea	Heathfield	
HAYGARTH Rev George/3	Henfield	Lindfield	Tory
INGRAM Hugh/13	Steyning	Southover & Brighton	Moderate Reformer
KNIGHT Charles	Worthing	Wivelsfield	
LEE Thomas/13	Horsham	Hurst-pierpoint	Tory
LEWIN Rev Spencer Js*/3	Ifield	Crawley	Tory
LINDFIELD George/12	Horsham	Ditcheling	Reformer
MARSHALL Charles	Steyning	Brighton	In ill health
MOORE James/12	Ifield	Crawley	voted contrary to the wishes of the Rector of the Parish
PENFOLD John/3	Steyning	Piecombe	a Tory
PICKARD Thomas/12	Rusper	Twineham	a Farmer uninfluenced
POWELL Henry/12	Chichester	Northiam	Liberal Reformer
POWELL James/12	Chichester	Northiam	Liberal Reformer
PRATT John/12	Steyning	Brighton	uninfluenced
RASON Samuel/12	Finden	E.Bourne	
READY John	Chichester	E. Grinstead	is Governor of the Isle of Man
SHELLEY Sir Timothy bart	Warnham	Worth	Supported Mr Cavendish on Account of his general fitness to represent the County
SKELTON Francis/12	New Shoreham	Brighton	
SMART Thomas/12	Horsham	Cliffe	Reformer
SMITH Edmund/13	Horsham	Hove	Tory
SMITH John	Chichester	Lindfield	M P for Buckingham

NAME	WHERE RESIDENT	WHERE REGISTERED	OBSERVATIONS
STEDMAN Deudney/1	Horsham	Barcombe	known to Mr Cav
STREET George/12	Warnham	Brighton	Reformer
SYMS Rev William	West Grin-	Ashburnham, Pevensey, Warbleton & Willingdon is a reformer the illness of Mrs Thornton his mother prevented him from going to the Poll	
THORNTON Thomas	Horshem	Brighton	
THORPE John sen/12	Horsham	Brighton	Reformer
TREDCROFT Henry/13	Warnham	Bolney	is well known to Mr Cavendish
TRIBE William	Worthing	Bolney	
TYLER William	Petworth	Burwash	
UPPERTON Luke/13	Thakeham	Bolney	Independent
WALLER James/13	Horsham	Bolney	Independent
WOOD Robert	Waterbeach	Brighton	
WOOD Robert/13	West-hampnett	Brighton	
WOODWARD Rev Packm. William	West Grinstead	Framfield	
WOOLGAR Josias/13	Steyning	Brighton	Uninfluenced

KENT - 123

The voters marked + are under the influence of the Proprietor of Erridge Castle or his Steward but those not marked are cheifly(sic) independent Freeholders.

ALCE Thomas/13	Wittersham	Winchelsea	
ATKINS Thomas	Hawkhurst	Salehurst	Rejected
AUSTEN Thomas/13	Sevenoaks	E. Guildeford	
AYERST Francis/3	Hawkhurst	Salehurst	
AYERST Thomas/23	Newenden	Ewhurst	
BACK John*/12	Brookland	Rye	
BARLING Isaac*/12	Brookland	Broomhill	
BARREN William	Rochester	Ticehurst	
BARROW Thomas/12	Hawkhurst	Dallington	
BARTON Harry	Goudhurst	Hailsham	
BATES William	Ivy Church	Peasmarsh	
BEALE William/1	T. Wells	Wadhurst	
BEECHAM William Pain*/3	Hawkhurst	Ewhurst	Mr Darbys Agent
BEECHING Thomas/12	Tonbridge	Lamberhurst	
BENNETT Edmund/13	T. Wells	Frant & Rotherfield	
BENNETT George+/12	T. Wells	Rotherfield	
BENNETT James+/1	T. Wells	Frant	

NAME	WHERE RESIDENT	WHERE REGISTERED	OBSERVATIONS
BLACKMAN William	*Rolvenden*	*Iden*	
BRENT John	*Canterbury*	*Keymer*	
BROOKE Rev John K S	*Eltham*	*Hurstperpoint*	
BRYANT John/12	Hawkhurst	Salehurst	
BURFORD Thomas/3	Minster Abbey	Heathfield	
BUTLER Thomas	*Ivy Church*	*Broomhill*	

Those marked with + are under the Influence of Lord
Abergavenny. Those not marked are Independent.

CARRUTHERS John	*Speldhurst*	*Frant*	
CLOAKE Thankful/12	Tenterden	Winchelsea	
COLLINGWOOD G Newnham	*Hawkhurst*	*Bodiam*	
COMBER William sen/12	Cowden	East Grinstead	
DEANE James/12	T. Wells	Newick	
DELVES Joseph/3	T. Wells	Rotherfield	
DELVES Thomas/3	T. Wells	Frant	
DELVES William+/1	T. Wells	Frant	
DUDLOW John/3	Westalling	Mayfield	
DURRANT John Mercer	*Hawkhurst*	*Salehurst*	*Rejected. Tendered for Mr Cavendish*
DURRANT Samuel Wood-gate	*Cranbrook*	*Salehurst*	*Rejected. Tendered for Mr Cavendish*
DURRANT Thomas/12	Hawkhurst	Salehurst	
DURRANT William	*Hawkhurst*	*Mayfield*	*Dead*
DYKE George Hart/3	Tonbridge	Waldron	
DYKE Percival Hart/3	Orpington	Bexhill	
EASTLAND William+	*T. Wells*	*Frant*	
EDWARDS John/12	Newenden	Northiam	
ELLIS James	*Barming*	*Burwash*	
ELLIS William	*Rootham*	*Brighton*	
FAGG Matthew*/12	Lydd	St Clement	
FARRANT John/12	Maidstone	Wadhurst	
FOREMAN Robert	*T. Wells*	*Rotherfield*	
FRANCIS John/12	Cranbrook	Udimore	
FRENCH George*/12	Hawkhurst	Salehurst	
FUGGLE John/12	Brenchley	Bexhill	
GAINSFORD Joseph/12	Cowden	Hartfield	
GALLOP William/2	Sandhurst	St Mary in the Castle	
GILLETT Richard/12	T. Wells	Frant	
GODFREY Thomas/12	Hawkhurst	Rye	
GRIST William/13	Brookland	Broomhill	
HANSON William/12	Newenden	Northiam	

NAME	WHERE RESIDENT	WHERE REGISTERED	OBSERVATIONS
HARDINGE Rev Sir Chas/3	Tonbridge	Crowhurst	Tory
HARMAN Anthony/3	Tonbridge	Salehurst	Tory
HARVEY Rev Thomas+/3	Cowden	Hartfield	
HILDER John	Sandhurst	Northiam	
HOBGOOD James	Loughton	Battle	
HOLLANDS Henry/12	Cowden	Westhoathly	
JEFFERY James Gardiner /12	Yalding	Westfield	
JONES John/13	Goudhurst	Lamberhurst	
JONES Rev Richard	Brasted	Frant	
JORDAN Rev Richard/13	Rochester	Mountfield	
KILLICK Anthony	Sunbridge	Frant	

Anthony Killick is a Bailiff or Land Steward under the Dyke Family who are strong Tories.

KNELL Benjamin+/12	T. Wells	Frant	
KNIGHT Edward	Godmersham	Kingston	Tory
LENEY Abraham	Rootham	Burwash	
LEVETT William	Wittersham	Bodiam	
LEWIS John Wenham	Westerham	St Clement	Whig
MARCHANT Thomas Bold/12	Brenchley	Lamberhurst	
MARTIN Fiennes Wykeham/3	Leeds Castle	Keymer & Peasmarsh	

Those marked + are under the influence of Lord Abergavenny.

MILES William/12	Tonbridge	Heathfield	
MISKIN John Thomas	Rochester	Mayfield	
MONEYPENNY James Isaac/3	Hadlow	E. Guildeford	
MONEYPENNY Thomas	Rolvenden	Peasmarsh	
MOON John	T. Wells	Rotherfield	
MORTIMER John/3	Lewisham	Iden	
NEALE Edward*+/12	T. Wells	Frant	
NEVILLE the Hon Rev W /13	Westmalling	Frant	
NORMAN Rev John Henry	Deal	Iden	Tory
NORMAN William George	Bromley	E.Grinstead	Tory
NORTON Owen	Horsmonden	Rye	Influenced by Sir William Geary the late Candidate for West Kent
NORTON Silas	Westmalling	Rye	Influenced by Sir William Geary the late Candidate for West Kent
NYE Henry	T. Wells	Hartfield	Ind. Whig
PACKER John	Woolwich	Brighton	
PAINE Daniel	Deptford	Battle	

NAME	WHERE RESIDENT	WHERE REGISTERED	OBSERVATIONS
PAINE Samuel/2	Sandhurst	Bodiam	
PAINE Thomas/12	Appledore	E. Guildford	
PARSONS Robert/2	Edenbridge	Worth	
PAYNE Thomas/12	Rolvenden	Burwash	
PAYNE William/12	Chevening	Westhoathly	
PEGG Harry+/12	T. Wells	Frant	
PELHAM Thomas/12	Kenardington	Iden	
PERKINS Frederick	*Chipstead*	*Brighton*	
POMFRET Virgil	*Tenterden*	*Iden*	
RUSSELL James	*Cranbrook*	*Rye*	
SLOMAN John	*T. Wells*	*Frant*	*Ind. Whig*
SMALLFIELD Thomas/12	Wittersham	Iden	
SMITH Richard	*Lewisham*	*Salehurst*	
SPRINGATE Richard/13	Goudhurst	Lamberhurst	
SPRINGETT Edmund/23	Hawkhurst	Salehurst	
SPRINGETT John/23	Hawkhurst	Salehurst	
STILEMAN Richard	*Greenwich*	*Peasmarsh & Winchelsea*	
STONE John	*T. Wells*	*Frant*	
STRINGER John*+/12	T. Wells	Frant	
TAPLEY William	*Brompton*	*Heathfield*	
TAYLOR Thomas+/12	T. Wells	Brighton	
THOMPSON Edward Pett	*Dover*	*Rye*	
TOLHURST Peter*/1	Snargate	Waldron	
TURNER Richard/12	Penshurst	Horsted Keynes	
WALTER Stephen	*Horsmonden*	*Hooe*	*Tory*
WATERMAN William	*Tenterden*	*Beckley*	*Tory*
WEDD George/12	Yalding	Bexhill	
WEDD James/12	Yalding	Bexhill	

Those not marked are Independent.

NAME	WHERE RESIDENT	WHERE REGISTERED	OBSERVATIONS
WEST Samuel+/12	T. Wells	Frant	
WHITE Samuel/12	Yalding	Salehurst	
WHITE Thomas/12	Yalding	E. Bourne	
WHITEHEAD John/2	Yalding	Rye	
WILMSHURST Adam/12	Brenchley	Lamberhurst	
WINCHESTER Henry	*Hawkhurst*	*Salehurst*	*Tory*
YEATES Grant David	*T. Wells*	*Withyham*	*Whig*
YOUNG Edward/3	Hawkhurst	Brede	

SURREY - 32

NAME	WHERE RESIDENT	WHERE REGISTERED	OBSERVATIONS
BROAD William	*Dorking*	*Cuckfield*	
BROOK Richard/12	Chiddingstone	E. Grinstead	

NAME	WHERE RESIDENT	WHERE REGISTERED	OBSERVATIONS
BROOKE Thompson Dan/12	Croydon	Brighton	
BURT Thomas	*Reigate*	*Worth*	
BYRNE Patrick	*Lingfield*	*E. Grinstead*	
CALVERLY Thomas/3	Ewell Castle	Hellingly	
CLUTTON William/13	Hartswood	Cuckfield	
COLQUHOUN Henry	*Guildford*	*Brighton*	
COMPTON Thomas	*Reigate*	*Worth*	
CONSTABLE James/12	Horley	Worth	
CRAWFORD William/1	Dorking	Brighton	
CROWLEY Charles Sedgwick	*Croydon*	*E. Grinstead*	
CRUNDEN Henry/12	Reigate	Cuckfield	
ELLIS Thomas/1	Catterham	E. Grinstead	
FOSKETT Joseph	*Reigate*	*Brighton*	
GREEN Philip	*Buxton*	*Hove*	
HARDY William Robert/12	Horne	Worth	
HARMAN John	*Croydon*	*Northiam*	
JAMES Joseph	*Hascombe*	*Buxted*	
JENNER James/12	Godstone	Worth	
KELSEY Robert/2	Lingfield	E. Grinstead	
MACKENZIE Rev William D D	*Hascombe*	*Brighton & Burwash*	
MARGESSON Rev Wm/13	Ockley	Whatlington	
MILLER James Francis*/12	Croydon	Brighton	
NEALE Thomas	Reigate	Worth	
ROBINSON Sanders William	*Reigate*	*Ardingly*	
STONE John/12	Godstone	E. Grinstead	
TURNER Charles Hampden	*Godstone*	*Lindfield*	
TURNER Edward/3	Reigate	Brighton	
WHITINGTON Peter	*Ripley*	*Brighton*	
WILKS Joseph Browne	*Godstone*	*Brighton*	
WILLIAMSON Joseph	*Guildford*	*Brighton*	

LONDON - 157

NAME	WHERE RESIDENT	REGISTERED
ALLEN William*/12	Stoke Newington	Lindfield
ALLEY William/1	Chiswell st.	Brighton
ALLFREY William	*36 Linc.Inn Flds.*	*Westham*
ALLISTON John	*38 Russel sq.*	*Brighton*
APPLEYARD Fred. Newman	*Cursitor's Office*	*Burwash*
APPLEYARD Richard Smith	*Bedford Square*	*Burwash*
ATKINSON Simmons Jas*/12	Minories	Seaford

NAME	WHERE RESIDENT	REGISTERED
ATLEE John Faulconer	Wandsworth	Brighton
BALDOCK Edward Holmes*/1	Hanways Oxf.s.	Buxted
BARNES Henry	Falcon ct. Boro'	Brighton
BARRY Charles Upham/3	41 Torrington s.	Little Horsted
BASS James/12	15 Circus s. Marl.	Brighton
BAYLEY Robert Riddell*/12	Basinghall street	St Mary in the Castle
BAYNTUM L C jun/13	Junr. U.S. Club	Clayton
BAYNTUM Samuel Adlam	Junr. U.S. Club	Cuckfield
BECKETT Burrows*/13	Chur. Row, Ald.	Lindfield
BELL Henry	10 Oxford st.	Brighton
BENSON Joseph	Hounslow	Ore
BERRY James sen/12	120 Aldersgate s.	Ringmer
BLICK Charles Tufton	15 Regent street	Brighton
BOSTOCK Ellis	41 Hunt. s. Brs. s.	Westhoathly
BRADSHAW William/12	N. Gal. Auc. Mart	Brighton
BROMLEY John/12	17 Commercial r.	Brighton
BRYANT William	St. George's Flds.	Lindfield
BURGOYNE Thomas John	160 Oxford str.	Battle
BURTENSHAW Henry/12	31 Leicester sq.	Ditcheling
BURTON Septimus	10 N. s. Linc. Inn	St Leonards & St My. Mag
CAPES John	Walworth	E. Grinstead
CARR John	16 New st. Newi.	Wadhurst
CAVENDISH Charles Compton	Burlington Hse.	Eastbourne
CAVENDISH George Henry	Belgrave Square	Westham
CAVENDISH Richard	Belgrave Square	Eastbourne
CAVENDISH Lord William	Belgrave Square	West Dean
CHASSEREAU James Daniel/12	9 Finsbury square	Brighton
CLEASBY Stephen	Old Broad street	Brighton
COBB George/13	Clements Inn	Brighton
COLEMAN Charles/12	Foley Pl. Maryle.	St Clement
COOPER Thos Poynton*/12	Upper Clapton	Brighton
CRAKE William	Nottinghill, Kenstn.	St Mary in the Castle
CRUTTENDEN William	31 Osbrg. st. Rt. Pk.	Salehurst
CUBITT Thomas	Laurence rd. Clap.	Brighton
CURLING Jesse	Bermondsey	E. Grinstead
DAVIDSON John/12	Cross ks. Wood st.	Brighton
DAVIES William/1	38 North Audley st.	Brighton
DAVIS William	106 Borough	Waldron
DAWES Thomas	Camberwell	Winchelsea

NAME	WHERE RESIDENT	REGISTERED
DENNE Richard/3	Inner Temple	Udimore
DENNE William John	*Doctors Commons*	*Udimore*
DODSON John	*Doctors Commons*	*Hurstperpoint*
DONNE Edward	5 New Inn	Battle
DOWLEY Frederick A*/1	Broad st. City	Worth
DOXAT Alexis James	*13 Bishopsgate st.*	*Ewhurst*
DURRANT John Mer.Boswl.	*Hammersmith*	*Southover*
EDMONDS Absalon	*53 Castle st. boro.*	*Rottingdean*
EGAN John*/2	58 Guildford street	Hove
ELLIOTT Charles jun/13	47 Portland place	Hove
EMLY Samuel	*St. Grmn. ter. Blkth.*	*Brighton*
FARNCOMB Thomas	*Harleyford. Kens.*	*St Mary in the Castle*
FINCH John	*31 Dean st. Soho*	*Rottingdean*
FITZGERALD John	*Portland place*	*Seaford*
FLANDERS William	*Hackney*	*Brighton*
FOLKARD Daniel	*14 London rd. boro.*	*Brighton*
FOLKER Samuel Shepherd	*2 Bridge st. West.*	*Brighton*
FRAZER George	*10 New sq. Linc. In.*	*St Leonards & St My Mag*
FULLER Augustus Elliott	*Cliford st. St Jams.*	*E. Grinstead*
GARRAWAY Abel/12	Durham p. Hackney	Worth
GOLDSMID Isaac Lyon/12	Dulwich H. Cambr.	Hove
GOTOBED Thomas	*82 Great Russell st.*	*Brighton*
GRAHAM Nathaniel	*Pinner*	*Brighton*
GREGSON John/3	Angel c. Throg. s.	Salehurst
GURNEY Samuel*/12	Lombard st.	Lindfield
HAMILTON Frederick	*Jermyn st.*	*Brighton*
HANLEY William*/1	Newington Green	Brighton
HANLEY William Lucas	*1 Furnival's Inn*	*Brighton*
HARLEY William	*New s. Kennington*	*Brighton*
HARRIS William*/12	50 High Holborn	Brighton
HARVEY Dan. Whittle	*George st. Westm.*	*St Michael & Brighton*
HARVEY James	*Old Kent Road*	*Brighton*
HESELTINE William	*Turret H.S. Lamb.*	*Southover*
HEWETSON Henry	*Turnham Green*	*Worth*
HOFFMAN John	*Han. Cres. Ret's. Pk.*	*Ewhurst*
HOLROYD John	*23 Northumber.s. Strand*	*Bolney & Barcombe*
IMPEY Elijah Barwell	*Clapham Common*	*Newick*
JACOB John	*Birchin lane*	*E. Grinstead*
JONES George	*Jermyn street*	*Brighton*
KAYE Joseph/13	Gower street	St Mary in the Castle

NAME	WHERE RESIDENT	REGISTERED
KILWICK Rev William	*St. Mary Axe.*	*Alciston*
LANE Thomas	*Russell square*	*E. Grinstead*
LEWIS Thomas	*Union Assur. Office*	*Brighton*
LONG Charles/12	16 Bath pl. Fitz. sq.	Hove
LUCAS William*/12	9 Butcher Hall lane	Horsted Keynes
LYON Joseph William	*27 Claremont sq.*	*Brighton*
MacWHINNIE William*/12	Pentonville	Brighton
MAITLAND John	*Bridge str. Westm.*	*Framfield*
MAITLAND Robert	*Middle Temple*	*Ringmer*
MARCHANT Michael/12	Field row, Clapham	Lindfield
MATTHEWSON Samuel	*Hounslow*	*Battle*
MEAKIN Thomas*/12	Norton Falgate	Brighton
MILNER Ralph*/12	4 Prospect pl. Boro'.	Worth
MOOREMAN Thomas/3	Lambeth	Bexhill
MORFEE William*/12	4 Geo. Terrace. O.Kt.r.	All Sts. Hastings
MURRAY William	*Grosvenor street*	*Hove*
NORTON Bradbury*/12	St Clement's Inn	Rye
NORTON Theodore	*St Clement's Inn*	*Rye*
OAK Thomas	*Greenwich*	*Brighton*
OGLE Sir Charles bart	*Belgrave square*	*Bexhill*
PALMER George*/12	12 Up. Woburn pl.	Brighton
PALMER Philip	*118 St Martin's la.*	*Brighton*
PARR William/3	Throgmorton street	E. Hoathly
PELHAM John Cressett	*Warren's Hotel*	*Crow. & St Michael*
PENFOLD Rv G Saxby D D/3		Rotherfield
PILCHER Jeremiah	*16 Russell square*	*Brighton*
PILCHER John Giles	*St Morgan's l. Boro'.*	*Brighton*
PILCHER William Humphrey	*18 New Broad str.*	*Brighton*
PODMORE Henry	10 Heathcote st. Meck. sq.	Clayton
PRICE Richard	*Duke st. West.*	*Withyam*
QUAIFE Thomas	*Somerset House*	*Battle*
RAWLINS George	*Castle st. Leicest. sq.*	*Bexhill*
RICHARDS Thomas/3	Sessions H. Clkwl.	Lindfield
ROPER David R	*11 Stamford street*	*Brighton*
RUSSELL Rev Whitworth	*Penitentiary Milbk.*	*Chiddingly*
SAUNDERS Thomas	*Great Surrey street*	*Hove*
SAVAGE Charles Augustus	*Fetter lane*	*Rotherfield*
SCARLETT Sir James knt	*4 New s. Sprg. Grds.*	*Saint John*
SCARLETT Robert C/13	1 Park st. Westm.	Chailey
SHAW William	*Kentish Town*	*Brighton*
SKILBECK John Joseph	*Islington*	*Brighton*

NAME	WHERE RESIDENT	REGISTERED
SMART Richard/13	Banner s. St Luke's	All Saints Lewes
SMITH John Abel	*Portland Place*	*Rotherfield*
SPARROW Jonathan	*Wandsworth Road*	*Brighton*
SPENCE Henry Hume	*Earl's ter. Kensngt.*	*Southmalling*
STOTT William/12	Peckham Rye lane	Lindfield
SUTTON Arthur White/12	Kennington	Brighton
TAYLOR Richard*/12	Red Lion ct. Fleet st.	All Sts. Hastings
TAYLOR William/12	Clapham	All Sts. Lewes
TERRY John		*Iden*
TERRY Thomas/12	29 Minories	Iden
THOMAS George/12	Chapel End, Walthamst.	Brighton
THOMPSON D Ibbetson/13	Kilburn Priory	Brighton
TUCKER Thomas	*5 Henrietta street*	*Brede*
TURNER Philip	*Lambs Conduit st.*	*Brighton*
WALKER Jas Kinlock/12	40 Drury lane	Brighton
WALKER Matt Clement/12	48 Skinner street	Brighton
WALKER Thomas	*Denmark h. Cambl.*	*Brighton*
WALLER John Champion/1	*8 Grv. s. Camden t.*	Cuckfield
WALLER Thos George/13	48 Gt.Russell st.Blooms.	Cuckfield
WALPOLE Edward	*12 Downing street*	*Northiam*
WALPOLE Robert	*7 Hanover square*	*Brighton*
WARREN Robert	*30 Strand*	*Brighton*
WESTALL William	*Cheapside*	*Burwash*
WILLIAMS Richard	*Stroud Gr. Hornsey*	*Brighton*
WILLIS John	*Essex st. Strand*	*St John*
WOOD James/3	422 Strand	Keymer
WOOD John	*St Barthlom. Hosp.*	*Keymer*
WOOD John Binns	*Clapham Road*	*Brighton*
WRIGHT John/12	Hampstead	E. Grinstead
WRIGHT William Consett	*Upper Clapton*	*Brighton*

DISTANT PLACES - 52

ADKINS Harry	*Warwick Gaol*	*Waldron*
BACCHUS George	*Birmingham*	*Brighton*
BAYNTON Rev Henry/3	*Devizes Wilts.*	Keymer
BELLAMY John	*Wisbeach, Camb.*	*Wadhurst*
BENNISON George	*Exeter*	*Brighton*
BINGHAM Rev Richard/3	Gosport	Seaford
BROWN Nicholas*/3	Chepstow, Monm.	Cliffe
CARR John	*Sewardstone, Essex*	*Brighton*
CAWSTON Thomas	*Buckinghamshire*	*Bodiam*
CLEMENT Jas Kinlock/12	Laytonstone, Essex	Brighton
CLEMENT James R	*Leytonstone, Essex*	*Brighton*
CLITHEROW James	*Brentford*	*Crawley*
COLBATCH Henry	*Dublin*	*Brighton*

94

NAME	WHERE RESIDENT	REGISTERED
CROWLEY Abraham/12	Alton, Hants.	E. Grinstead
CROWLEY Henry	Alton, Hants.	E. Grinstead
DARBY Horatio D'Estre	Leap Castle, Ireland	Warbleton
DILLWYN Lewis William	Penlargan Glam	Brighton
DORSET Henry/12	Freshwater IOW	Ashburnham
DUCANE Henry	Witham Essex	Brighton
ELLIOTT Edward B	Tusford Notts	Hove
ELLIS Thomas/3	Bath	Hove
FREWEN Moreton	Cheavly Gr. Suffolk	Northiam
GINN Benjamin	Weeden Northam.	Brgtn & St Clem
GOLEBORN Thos Lynch	Peats Hill, Bedford	Brighton
GOODE Henry	Ryde IOW	Brighton
GORDON William	Broomwich Staff	Bexhill
HANSON Rev Joshua F	Backwell, Somers	Brighton
HARCOURT Geo. Simon	Ankerwyche, Bucks	E. Grinstead
HARPER Joseph James	Blidlow Ris. Bucks	All Sts. Hstgs.
HAWKINS Rev Edw. D D	Oriel Col. Oxford	Lamberhurst
HENNIKER John	Thornham, Suffolk	Withyam
HOLFORD Robert	Niton IOW	Maresfield
JORDAN Gibbes Walker	Waterstock, Oxfds.	Rye
LARKIN Edmund Robert	Oxford	Brighton
MARTEN Frederick/12	Leiston, Suffolk	St John
MORRIS George*/12	Gosfield, Essex	Battle
NICHOLL Samuel John	Lyndhurst, Hants.	Mountfield
OLLNEY John Harvey	Cheltenham	Brighton
PARKINSON John	Waltham Cross, Chesh.	Burwash
PENNEFATHER Edward	Dublin	Hooe
PROSSER James	Loudwater, Berks	Rye
RIES J M/13	Swanwitch, Dorset	Brighton
RILEY William Felix	Frst. Hill, Clwr. Bk.	All Sts. Hstgs.
SHAW George	Manchester	Brighton
SLATER James Henry	Lausanne, Switz.	Newick
SOAMES Henry	Broadfield, Herts.	Hove
SPINK John	Froyle, Hants.	St My. Mag.
UNWIN Edward	Sutton in Ash. Notts.	Iden
VALLANCE Charles	Chippenham, Wilts.	Brighton
WATSON Hon. Henry	Hemelhamp. Hants.	Laughton
WHEELER Robert	Aylesbury, Berks.	All Sts. Lewes

INDEX

NAME	PAGE	NAME	PAGE
CAMDEN	34(2),48,58, 75(2), 76(7)	CHAPMAN	12(2),28(2), 38,43,77
		CHAPPELL	83
CAMERON	74,84	CHARLWOOD	28
CAMFIELD	66	CHASEMAR	84
CAMP	12	CHASSEREAU	12,91
CAMPANY	69	CHATFIELD	5(5),12,46, 54,57
CAMPBELL	11		
CAMPION	46,54	CHATTERTON	67(2)
CANE	18,65(2)	CHEALE	55,74
CAPES	91	CHEESMAN	12(4),18,34(2)
CAPLIN	25	CHELOW	19
CAPPER	82	CHERRY	24
CARD	34,57	CHEWTER	83
CARE	62	CHICHESTER	8,22(2),32(7), 44,49(7),63(2) 70,72
CAREY	36,47(3),49		
CARLETON	51		
CARNEGIE	70	CHILD	4,72
CARPENTER	22(2)	CHILDRENS	12
CARR	32,34,91,94	CHITTENDEN	12
CARRUTHERS	87	CHOYCE	12
CARTER	12(2),53,57,63 81	CHRISMAS	21,42(2),75
		CHRISTFORD	6
CATT	10,12,64,79(3)	CHRISTMAS	6
CAVE	32,84	CLAPSON	43,43,44,72
CAVENDISH(CAV)	1(3),2(5),3(2) 4,5,7(2),9,13 18,19(2),20(2) 23,25(2),27, 28,29(2),31,34 37(2),40(4), 47,53,57,58,59 61,73(7),76, 78,81,83(3), 84(2),85,86(2) 87(2),91(4)	CLARE	36
		CLARK	13,28,67(3)
		CLARKE	34
		CLATON	31
		CLEAR	51
		CLEASBY	91
		CLEMEN	94
		CLEMENT	40,94
		CLIFFORD	81
		CLITHEROW	94
		CLOAKE	87
CAVIE	34	CLOKE	36(2)
CAWSTON	94	CLUTTON	90
CHAFFEY	12	COALMAN	9
CHALK	12	COATSWORTH	32
CHAMBERLAYNE	67	COBB	91
CHAMBERS	42,70	COBBY	13
CHAMPION	70	COCHRAN	66
CHANDLER	12,40,46,83	COCKETT	6(2)
CHAPLIN	12	COE	20

NAME	PAGE	NAME	PAGE
FREDERICK	26	GEST	51
FREEMAN	13,44,51	GIBB	5(2)
FRENCH	22,26,68,72,76	GIBBON	68
	87	GIBBS	6,50,61,76
FREWEN	95	GILBERT	8(3),19,20,
FRIEND	32		25(4),26(3),
FRISE	68		27(5),32(3),
FRY	57(5)		57,61,76
FRYMAN	68	GILES	68
FUGGLE	87	GILFIN	36(2)
FULCHER	28(2)	GILHAM	83
FULLER	5(2),8(2),	GILL	68,79
	18(4),21,32,37	GILLAUME	85
	42(5),43(2),44	GILLETT	87
	45(2),49,60,63	GILLON	44(2),45(3),
	71,72(2),78(3)		36
	82,83,92	GINN	95
FULLJAMES	34	GLAISYER	13
FUNNELL	5,22,71	GLANDFIELD	40
FURNER	11(3),13,40	GLANVILLE	72(2)
GAGE	8(2),34,54,56,	GOBLE	42
	79(2),80(4)	GODDARD	64
GAINSFORD	23,87	GODDEN	70
GALLARD	13	GODFREY	10,87
GALLOP	40,87	GOFFE	14
GANSDEN	6	GOLDFINCH	4(2),52
GARDENER	27	GOLDSMID	92
GARDINER	76	GOLDSMITH	18,22,36,54,55
GARDNER	28		76,77
GARLAND	42	GOLDSTON	49
GARNER	6,30,69	GOLEBORN	95
GARNHAM	51,52	GOOD	14
GARRATT	13	GOODALL	14
GARRAWAY	92	GOODDAY	32
GASSON	37	GOODE	95
GASSTON	56	GOODMAN	47
GATES	51	GOODWIN	6,44
GAUNT	32	GOODYER	51
GEALL	65	GOORD	32
GEAR	52(2)	GORDON	8,60(2),61,95
GEARY	88(2)	GORHAM	44
GEERE	43	GORING	5,21,42(2),43,
GEERING	5,36,51,80(4)		74
GELL	50,85	GORRING	70(2)
GEORGE	39		

NAME	PAGE	NAME	PAGE
HEATHFIELD	26,69,76	HOLLAWAY	18(2)
HEATHURLY	26	HOLLINGDALE	64
HEAVER	28,48,71	HOLLIS	68
HELE	11	HOLLOWAY	68
HELMSLEY	33	HOLMAN	20,22(3),37,44
HEMSLEY	20,32,33		46,47,76(2)
HENBREY	45	HOLMDEN	54
HENLY	31(2)	HOLMES	57
HENNIKER	37,95	HOLROYD	6,92
HENTY	19	HOLT	82
HEPBURN	21(2)	HOMAN	39(2)
HESELTINE	92	HOMEWOOD	33,35,83
HESSELL	68	HONEYSETT	19,24,68
HEWETSON	92	HONISS	41(2)
HEWETT	31(2)	HONNISETT	44
HICK	20,50	HOOKE	56
HICKMOTT	35,49	HOOKER	19,28,37,67,
HICKS	42,50,51,68,78		83(2)
HIDE	4(2),22(2)	HOOPER	23
HIDER	47,66	HOPE	14
HILDER	21,31,36,59,61	HOPER	50(5),53,55,62
	68,69(8),		64(2)
	70(10),76,88	HOPPS	14
HILDERA	5	HORTON	62
HILL	8,14,37,46,56	HOSMAN	57
HILLMAN	51(3),54,80	HOTHER	50(3)
HILLS	27,33	HOUNSOME	28
HILTON	3	HOW	69,74
HINKLEY	39(2)	HOWE	19
HISTED	28	HOWELL	35,42,46
HOAD	14,47(2)	HUGGETT	28,42(2),54,64
HOARE	28,33	HUGGINS	68
HOBBS	14	HUGHES	14,33
HOBDEN	21,24,42,54	HUMMITT	28
HOBGOOD	88	HUMPHREY	5,14(2),44,84
HODD	14,64	HUMPHREYS	55
HODE	36	HUNT	6,43,77,80
HODGE	73	HUNTER	68
HODSON	10,14,20,27,81	HUNTLEY	48,73
HOEY	51(2)	HURDIS	74
HOFFMAN	92	HURLEY	48,53,55,65
HOLDEN	14,53	HURLY	48,72
HOLFORD	14,59,95	HURSELL	57
HOLLAND	9,60(2),63,78	HURST	26(4)
HOLLANDS	8,64,88	HUSSELL	26

NAME	PAGE	NAME	PAGE
WATSON	20,74,95	WICKHAM	47
WATTS	7(2),50,53	WIGNEY	6,18(3),46
WAYMARK	27	WILDISH	56,63
WEAVER	17	WILDS	18
WEBB	38,80	WILEMAN	24
WEBBER	5,47	WILKINS	32
WEBSTER	6(2),7(4),27	WILKS	90
WEDD	89,89	WILLARD	18,26(2),27(4)
WEEDEN	65		32,54,59,60,
WEEKES	47(2)		82(2)
WEEKS	70	WILLE	51,52(2)
WELCH	36	WILLIAMS	18,39(2),52,94
WELLER	7,18,36(3),43,	WILLIAMSON	41,90
	44,55,56,59,	WILLIS	94
	65(2),70,80	WILLSHER	31
WELLERD	39	WILMSHURST	78,89
WELLS	24,30(2),47,83	WILSON	33,47,67,69(2)
WELSFORD	18	WIMARK	62
WENHAM	78,79	WIMBLE	39,51
WEST	18,45,55,82,89	WINCH	4,63,74
WESTALL	94	WINCHESTER	20,43,45(2),89
WESTGATE	6,8	WINDUS	54
WESTON	20,21,22,51,52	WINGFIELD	38,41
	57,59(3),70,	WINGHAM	18
	71(2)	WINN	56
WESTOVER	18	WINSER	36
WETHERALL	72	WINTER	10,20,38,41,52
WETHERELL	30(4),31,72(5)	WINTON	30
	73(7),74(5)	WISDEN	18
WHAPHAM	49	WISDOM	35
WHATLEY	37	WISE	48
WHEELER	33,39,95	WOOD	5,18(2),19,
WHICHELO	18		20(3),23(2),24
WHITE	8,22,38,43,74,		25,28,30,31,33
	89(2)		38,39,41,49,
WHITEHEAD	89		51(2),56(2),
WHITEMAN	23,54,78,80,81		61(2),69(2),77
WHITFELD	51		86(2),94(3)
WHITFIELD	32	WOODHAMS	4(2),18,41,56,
WHITING	38		75,79,81
WHITINGTON	90	WOODMAN	72,81
WICKENDEN	66(2)	WOODROFFE	61
WICKENS	20,35,66(6),	WOODS	40
	67(4)	WOODWARD	22,33,34,42,56
WICKERSON	30		59,75,86

NAME	PAGE	NAME	PAGE
WOOLETT	33	WRENCH	70
WOOLGAR	43,86	WRENN	21(2),60
WOOLLET	62	WRIGH	18
WOOLLETT	69	WRIGHT	53,69,94(2)
WOOLLGAR	51	WYATT	61
WOOLVEN	24	WYBOURNE	8
WORDSWORTH	20	WYNN	44
WORGE	7,18	YATES	61
WORRELL	30	YEATES	18,89
WORSELL	69	YOUNG	10,11,33,42,43
WRATTEN	45(2)		45,70,71,84,89
WREN	20,30		

****

FUTURE PUBLICATIONS FROM PBN

EASTBOURNE, SUSSEX: MARRIAGES(St.Mary's) 1754-1837
A Transcription of the Registers.
EASTBOURNE, SUSSEX: BAPTISMS(St.Mary's) 1558-1837:

Part 2: E to K	Part 3: L to Q
Part 4: R to S	Part 5: T to Z

A Transcription of the Registers formulated alphabetically.
EASTBOURNE, SUSSEX: BURIALS(St.Mary's) 1558 - 1837)
A Transcription of the Registers.
EASTBOURNE, SUSSEX: CENSUS RETURNS FOR 1861
A Transcription of the census returns.
SUSSEX POLL BOOK OF 1820
Name,abode,occupier,freehold & vote cast.
HASTINGS, SUSSEX: GAOL RECORDS : 1842-1853
Name, age, offence & sentence. This will consist of two books.
HASTINGS, SUSSEX: UNION MARRIAGE APPLICATIONS: 1837-1879
A partial transcription giving most details.
HASTINGS, SUSSEX: RATE BOOK FOR 1826
Name,address & rate value.
HASTINGS, SUSSEX: WARD LIST FOR 1835
Name,address & property.
BRIGHTON, SUSSEX: RATE BOOK FOR 1826
Name,address,valuation & remarks.
MILITIA LIST OF OFFICERS - SUSSEX, HAMPSHIRE, KENT & SURREY: 1804
NOTE: ALL ABOVE BOOKS WILL BE EITHER INDEXED OR IN INDEX FORM.

FAMILY ROOTS
FAMILY HISTORY SOCIETY
(EASTBOURNE & DISTRICT)

JUDITH KINNISON BOURKE

Genealogist, Lecturer and Tutor
in Family & Local History

Why not join our Family History
Society?

Meetings held monthly. Speakers on
various aspects of Family History
& Members' Evenings arranged.

Monumental Inscriptions, Parish
Registers and other local
interest material published by
the group.

Full details available, with SAE
please, from:
The Secretary, Family Roots FHS,
22 Abbey Road, Eastbourne,
East Sussex. BN20 8TE.

Like to know how to trace the history of your family?

The History of Your House or Family can be traced.
If you would like to know more write to :

JUDITH KINNISON BOURKE
Rose Cottage
Chapel Row
Herstmonceux
Hailsham
East Sussex BN27 1RB (0323 832218)

Enclosing a S.A.E.
Member of the Association of Genealogists
and Record Agents

PBN   PUBLICATIONS

22 ABBEY ROAD, EASTBOURNE, EAST SUSSEX, BN20 8TE.

1801 CENSUS RETURNS
TICEHURST, Sussex.
1821 CENSUS RETURNS
HARTFIELD, Sussex.
CHIDDINGLY, Sussex.
HAILSHAM, Sussex.
1831 CENSUS RETURNS
ST. CLEMENT, HASTINGS, Sussex.
EAST DEAN & FRISTON, Sussex.
ST. JOHN SUB CASTRO, LEWES, Sussex.
TICEHURST, Sussex.
UCKFIELD, Sussex.
HAILSHAM, Sussex.
1821 & 1831 CENSUS RETURNS
ST. MARY-IN-THE-CASTLE, HASTINGS, Sussex.
1811 CENSUS & OTHER LISTS
ST. MICHAEL, LEWES, Sussex. Includes:- Population -
1811, Jury List, Voter's List circa 1832
CREW MEMBERS OF SHIPS TRADING FROM NEWHAVEN
BETWEEN 1864-1889
Name, age, occupation and place of origin. Indexed.
EWHURST HOUSEHOLDERS IN 1863
WITHYHAM INHABITANTS IN 1838
Details of families with some personal annotations.
SUSSEX MILITIA LISTS
Southern Division of Pevensey Rape(1803)
Northern Division of Pevensey Rape(1803)
Burwash(1831),Pevensey(1810)&Rottingdean(1797)
SUSSEX ENROLMENTS UNDER THE NAVY ACTS(1795+1797)

EASTBOURNE WAR MEMORIAL 1914-1918
Lists each man's name, occupation, when he died and ref.
EASTBOURNE MARRIAGES(St.Mary's Church) 1558-1753
Transcript of register. (Indexed)
EASTBOURNE BAPTISMS(St.Mary's Church) 1558-1837
Part 1: A to D. Transcript of register.
HASTINGS GAOL RECORDS
Commitments to Prison 1832-1841
HASTINGS REGISTERED ELECTORS 1836-7
Name, trade and employer. Indexed.

Prices on request with S.A.E. to: 22 Abbey Road,
Eastbourne, East Sussex BN20 8TE.